EUROPEAN DEFENCE
Meeting the strategic challenge

Peter Truscott

30-32 Southampton St
London WC2E 7RA
Tel: 020 7470 6100
Fax: 020 7470 6111
postmaster@ippr.org.uk
www.ippr.org
Registered charity 800065

The Institute for Public Policy Research is an independent charity whose purpose is to contribute to public understanding of social, economic and political questions through research, discussion and publication. It was established in 1988 by leading figures in the academic, business and trade-union communities to provide an alternative to the free market think tanks.

IPPR's research agenda reflects the challenges facing Britain and Europe. Current programmes cover the areas of economic and industrial policy, Europe, governmental reform, human rights, defence, social policy, the environment and media issues.

Besides its programme of research and publication, IPPR also provides a forum for political and trade union leaders, academic experts and those from business, finance, government and the media, to meet and discuss issues of common concern.

Trustees

Lord Eatwell (Chairman)
Gail Rebuck (Secretary)
Lord Gavron (Treasurer)
Lord Alli
Professor Tony Atkinson
Professor Kumar Bhattacharyya
Rodney Bickerstaffe
Lord Brooke
John Edmonds

Professor Anthony Giddens
Jeremy Hardie
Lord Hollick
Jane Humphries
Professor David Marquand
Frances O'Grady
Chris Powell
Jan Royall
Baroness Young of Old Scone

Production & design by **EMPHASIS**
ISBN 1 86030 142 8
© IPPR 2000
Printed and bound in Great Britain by Biddles Ltd, *www.biddles.co.uk*

Contents

Preface
List of acronyms
Acknowledgements
About the author

Introduction – the European defence debate   1

I: **TAKING A LEAD IN ENHANCING EUROPEAN DEFENCE CAPABILITIES**
European defence – the background   16
US attitudes to European defence   31
Conclusions and policy recommendations   36

II: **FOCUSING ON CAPABILITIES**
Some early criteria   38
The Revolution in Military Affairs (RMA)   45
Conclusions and policy recommendations   51

III: **CONSOLIDATION, GLOBALISATION AND TRANSATLANTIC RELATIONS**
Defence consolidation and globalisation   54
European defence integration and restructuring   61
Fortress Europe vs Fortress America   70
Conclusions and policy recommendations   83

IV: **PROCUREMENT ISSUES**
European armaments co-operation   86
Smart procurement, competition and European harmonisation   89
Conclusions and policy recommendations   96

V: **DEFENCE DIVERSIFICATION, INDUSTRIAL STRATEGY AND INNOVATION IN THE UK AND REGIONS**
Defence diversification, innovation and the supply chain   100
The regions   107
Conclusions and policy recommendations   109

VI: **A NEW STRATEGIC GOAL FOR EUROPE**
A holistic approach to EU defence   112
Moving towards common defence   123

Select bibliography   125

Preface

Why is the EU developing its own autonomous defence capability and why should the centre-left be taking these developments seriously? These are the questions that IPPR wants to see aired and we hope that Peter Truscott's report will prompt thinking and debate across a range of difficult issues.

The EU was set up with a set of key political goals that had at their core the prevention of future conflict in Europe. The stability and prosperity of western Europe now stands in sharp contrast to the economic problems of eastern Europe and a decade of conflict in the former Yugoslavia. It was the relative failure of the EU to deal with this conflict and its continued reliance on the US to show political and military leadership that catalysed key European players into thinking once again about the scope for the EU to act in its own right in dealing with conflicts, and the causes of conflicts, on its own doorstep.

A vision of a united, prosperous and stable Europe should be central to the goals of the centre-left across the continent. Although the main focus should be political and economic development leading eventually to enlargement of the EU, having the ability to deploy peacekeeping and peacemaking forces, including civilian police contingents, is critically important in achieving stability. However, this commitment raises key questions for the centre-left.

Peter Truscott argues that EU member states should commit themselves to spending an average of two per cent of GDP on defence if the aspirations for an independent defence capability are to be met. This would be needed to remedy the shortfalls in equipment, logistics and other areas exposed by the conflict in Kosovo. This target will be hard for many countries to meet alongside the claims on resources for health, education, social security and other key components of the welfare state that all governments, but especially those on the centre-left, see as priorities.

At a time when there is concern about the detachment of the elite from broad public opinion, Europe's political leaders also need to articulate more clearly the precise circumstances in which they expect that the EU will need to go it alone in military terms. They need to prepare the ground for explaining to the public why more resources should go into defence rather than say health or pensions. And to put it most starkly, they need to prepare for the day when British, French and German soldiers fight and perhaps get killed under an EU flag. Is public opinion in Europe ready for this?

The development of the EU's new defence capability will require changes in defence procurement practices and further consolidation in the defence industry. It is not clear whether the British government has yet 'joined up' its aspirations for developing this capability with its procurement process. Few MoD procurement decisions appear to have been affected by this new commitment. Any consolidation will also be painful, especially for those regions in the UK more dependent on defence contracts. These issues are also tackled in this report.

Strictly speaking policy makers should care first and foremost about having the defence capability needed to deliver policy objectives, and secondly delivering that capability at the lowest cost. The implications for the defence industry are of second-order importance. In practice, the politics of defence jobs means that no government is indifferent to the employment implications of defence procurement decisions. However, we should be wary of allowing the development of a European defence capability to be driven by the perceived need of European defence contractors to compete with their American counterparts.

Overall, this report is designed to spark debate on a series of difficult issues. The heart of the dilemma for the centre-left is the perennial problem of resource allocation. Alongside the commitment to the welfare state and indeed to improving foreign aid flows, how much are we prepared to pay for a European defence capability when no one even amongst Europe's political elite seems sure when and where it will ever be deployed?

Peter Robinson
IPPR

List of acronyms

ALCM	Air-Launched Cruise Missiles
AMRAAM	Advanced Medium-Range Air-to-Air Missile
BVRAAM	Beyond Visual Range Air-to-Air Missile
C2	Command and Control
C3	Command, Control and Communications
C3I	Command, Control, Communications and Intelligence
C3ISR	Command, Control, Communications, Intelligence. Surveillance and Reconnaissance
C4ISR	Command, Control, Communications, Computers, Intelligence, Surveillance and Reconnaissance
CDP	Common Defence Policy
CESDP	Common European Security and Defence Policy
CFIUS	Committee on Foreign Investment in the United States
CFSP	Common Foreign and Security Policy
CJPHQ	Combined Joint Permanent Headquarters
CJTF	Combined Joint Task Force
COTS	Commercial-off-the-shelf
CSI	Commercial Satellite Imagery
DCI	Defence Capabilities Initiative
DDA	Defence Diversification Agency (UK)
DERA	Defence Evaluation and Research Agency (UK)
DESO	Defence Export Services Organisation (UK)
DETR	Department of the Environment, Transport and the Regions (UK)
DFID	Department for International Development
DoD	Department of Defence (US)
DoP	Declaration of Principles (Anglo-US agreement)
DSACEUR	Deputy Supreme Allied Commander Europe
DSB	Defence Science Board (US)
DTI	Department of Trade and Industry (UK)
EAA	European Armaments Agency
EADC	European Aerospace and Defence Company
EADS	European Aeronautic Defence and Space Company
ECJSC	European Combined Joint Staff College
EJIC	European Joint Intelligence Committee
EMC	European Military Committee
EMU	European and Monetary Union
ERRF	European Rapid Reaction Force
ESDI	European Security and Defence Identity
ESDR	European Strategic Defence Review
EU	European Union
FLA	Future Large Aircraft
FCO	Foreign and Commonwealth Office (UK)
FDI	Foreign Direct Investment
FOCI	Foreign Ownership, Control or Influence
GCCS	Global Command and Control System
GDP	Gross Domestic Product

GOs	Government Offices (for the UK regions)
GPS	Global Positioning System
IFOR	Implementation Force, Bosnia
ISR	Intelligence, Surveillance and Reconnaissance
ITAR	International Traffic in Arms Regulations
KFOR	Kosovo Force
LOI	Letter of Intent
LRPS	Long-Range Precision Strike
MBT	Main Battle Tank
MC	Military Committee
MOU	Memorandum of Understanding
MRC	Major Regional Conflict
MS	Military Staff
MTW	Major Theatre War
NATO	North Atlantic Treaty Organisation
NGO	Non-Governmental Organisation
NDP	National Disclosure Policy
NMD	National Missile Defence
NSSG	New Strategic Security Goal
MoD	Ministry of Defence (UK)
OCCAR	Organisation Conjointe de Cooperation en Matiere d'Armament
OSCE	Organisation for Security and Cooperation in Europe
PGM	Precision Guided Munition
PPU	Policy Planning and Early Warning Unit (EU)
PSC	Political and Security Committee
PSO	Peace Support Organisation
RRHA	Rapid Reaction Humanitarian Agency
R & D	Research and Development
RBA	Revolution in Business Affairs
RMA	Revolution in Military Affairs
R & T	Research and Technology
SDI	Strategic Defence Initiative
SDR	Strategic Defence Review (UK)
SHAPE	Supreme Headquarters Allied Powers Europe
SFOR	Stabilisation Force, Bosnia
SME	Small and Medium-sized Enterprise
SPI	Smart Procurement Initiative
SSA	Special Security Agreement
TEU	Treaty on European Union
TLAM	Tomahawk land-Attack Missiles
UAV	Unmanned Aerial Vehicles
UN	United Nations
UNSC	United Nations Security Council
WEAG	Western European Armaments Group
WEAO	Western European Armaments Organisation
WEU	Western European Union
WMD	Weapons of Mass Destruction

Acknowledgements

This publication is the result of a research project undertaken between September 1999 and October 2000. It ranges across a number of issues connected with European defence, including defence capabilities, security doctrines, peacekeeping, defence consolidation, globalisation, procurement, defence diversification, industrial strategy, innovation, the regions, supply chains and a new strategic goal for Europe. There are policy recommendations for the EU and its institutions, for the US government (on opening the defence market) and there are a number for the British Government and its departments. The recommendations outline what the EU must do if it wants to achieve its goal of making Europe stronger. The UK must play its part, both as part of the EU and domestically, to enhance European defence and peacekeeping capabilities, strengthen its industrial base and develop an effective civilian crisis management capability.

Over the past year, I have received an enormous amount of help from a great many people. I would like to thank Matthew Taylor, Director of the IPPR, for giving me the idea to undertake the project, and for his support and advice throughout. Jess Tyrrell, Esther McCarthy, Peter Robinson (who gave good advice and looked at the text) and Helena Scott (Publications Manager) gave significant help during the course of the project. Beyond the IPPR, Peter McLoughlin at BAE Systems, Charles Blundell and Charles Coltman at Rolls-Royce, Jon Dennison and Graham Cole at GKN, Peter McKee (MD Raytheon UK) and Jackie Berger at Raytheon, and Roger Lyons and John Wall of MSF, all gave generously of their time and insights. The project could not have been conducted without the financial support of MSF, Raytheon, GKN, Rolls-Royce and BAE Systems. John Weston, CEO of BAE Systems, was kind enough to meet with me to discuss the project at Farnborough.

I have received tremendous input and support from Whitehall, NATO, the European Commission and the WEU Assembly. Lord Robertson, Secretary-General of NATO, Geoff Hoon MP, Secretary of State for Defence, and Baroness Symons of Vernham Dean, Defence Procurement Minister, have all shown very welcome interest in the ongoing work of the project. Andrew Hood and Alasdair McGowan, Special Advisers in the MoD, and David Clark, Special Adviser in the FCO, have also been helpful. I am grateful to input from Roger Liddle in the No 10 Policy Unit, and from Robert Cooper in the Cabinet Office. Dr Julian Lindley-French (of the WEU Institute for Strategic Studies), Admiral Gilles Cambarieu and Colin Cameron, Clerk to the WEU Assembly, provided me with invaluable information on a visit to Paris, and subsequently. Professor Keith Hayward of the Society of British Aerospace Companies gave me a wealth of information on the aerospace sector, and copies of several of his excellent papers. Dr Derek Braddon, Research Director of the Research Unit in Defence Economics, University of the West of England, provided me with his insights into the supply chain on visits to Bristol and Brighton. Michael Bell, Group Head of Strategic Analysis at BAE Systems provided me with a stimulating article on procurement and an informative meeting. Field Marshal Lord Vincent and General Sir Rupert Smith (DSACEUR), at meetings in London and Mons, gave me the considerable benefit of their experience, as did Dr Gunter Burghardt, Director-General for External Affairs at the European Commission in Brussels. Edgar Buckley, Assistant Secretary General for Defence Planning and Operations, filled me in on NATO issues.

Sir Robert Walmsley (Chief of Defence Procurement) provided interesting information on procurement issues, while Tony Edwards did the same on exports for DESO. Professor Damien McDonnell gave a full briefing on the work of the DDA, and I was also pleased to meet John Hunt (Director Aerospace and Defence Industries Policy) at the DTI, Richard Hatfield (Director of Policy) MoD, Adam Thomson (Head of Security Dept) FCO, and Ian Lee, Director Europe (MoD). On my visit to Washington DC, I received a great deal of help and advice from Bob Fitch and his BAE Systems office, and Barry New of Rolls-Royce. There I met, amongst others, the Hon David Oliver, Principal Deputy Under Secretary of Defense for Acquisition and Technology in the Pentagon; Dr John Hamre, President and CEO of the Centre for Strategic & International Studies and former Deputy Under Secretary of Defense and Dr Bill Schneider, former Under Secretary of State and BAE Systems NA Board Member; John Douglass, President of the Aerospace Industries Association of America; Robin Beard of Raytheon, and former NATO Assistant Secretary General; Marshall Billingsea, of the Senate Foreign Relations Committee; Walker Roberts, House International Relations Committee, and Jonathan Moore, of the Speaker's Policy Office. Francis Cevasco, Vice President of Hicks and Associates, filled me in on the Defence Science Board Task Force report and others matters; while Steve McCarthy (Attache Defence Supply) of the British Defence Staff in the British Embassy gave me a good deal of useful information on transatlantic trade issues.

Over the past year, I have interviewed, briefed and met many people to discuss the project, and others have also attended the two IPPR seminars held on the subject of European defence in June and September of this year. Bruce George MP (Chair, House of Commons Defence Select Committee) and Matthew Taylor were kind enough to chair the two seminars. I would also like to thank: Andy Head (Director, Marketing and Defence Systems), Raytheon; Martin Lee (Director of Business Strategy and Development) Rolls-Royce plc; Chris Peining, European Parliament, Head of UK Office; Geoff Martin, Head of UK representation, European Commission; Peter Carter, Head of Research, MSF; Tony McWalter MP; Richard Balfe MEP; Gary Titley MEP; Christian Leffler, Chris Patten's cabinet; Paul Dowdall, Senior Research Fellow, Research Unit in Economics, University of the West of England; Sue Bishop (Deputy Director, Defence Industries Policy), DTI; Peter Brown (Director of Marketing and Commercial) Rolls-Royce; Sally Hosseini (Principal Business Analyst) Rolls-Royce;

Robin Niblett, Vice-President of Strategic Studies, CSIS; Tony Pawson, Director General, DESO; Paul Busquet de Caumont, MD Aerospatiale Matra UK Ltd; Ian Stopps, Chief Executive, Lockheed Martin UK Ltd; Dr Maria Teresa Oxenstierna (Director, European Strategy) Raytheon; Giancarlo Chevallard (Head of Unit, Security Issues) European Commission; David Barnes, Chief Executive, Thomson Thorn Missile Electronics Ltd; Fred Cahill, Managing Director (Communications Division, Racal Defence Electronics); Stephen Scott, Research Dept, MSF; Joe Baynes (Director of Government Affairs and Business Development), Lockheed Martin UK Ltd; Richard Wigley, Business Development Manager, Alvis Vehicles Ltd; and George Eynon, Deputy Director of the Defence Manufacturers Association. I would also like to thank both the Society of British Aerospace Companies and Rolls-Royce for permission to reproduce some of their graphics in the report.

However, despite all the tremendous input, I take sole responsibility for the report's contents.

Finally, I would like to thank my patient wife, Svetlana, who had to endure over a month of me disappearing into the study to write.

About the author

Peter Truscott is Visiting Research Fellow with IPPR and a former Member of the European Parliament where he was Labour's Foreign Affairs and Defence spokesperson. He was also Vice-President of the Security and Disarmament sub-committee, and a member of the delegation to the WEU and North Atlantic Assembly. Latterly he has worked for the OSCE and as a senior expert with the European Commission. Following his doctorate from Oxford University, he has written extensively on foreign and security policy, including his book *Russia First* on post-Soviet Russia.

Introduction– the European defence debate

Introduction

This report is designed to look at the future of European defence. Although the EU has made great strides forward in agreeing to establish a European Rapid Reaction Force (ERRF) by 2003, there is still no agreement in the EU or in British government circles where the defence initiative is meant to be leading. Where will Europe be in defence terms in 2015 and 2030, and will the political elites of the EU be successful in taking public opinion along with them?

The report makes recommendations in all these areas, outlining the case for a New Strategic Security Goal (NSSG) for Europe, setting benchmarks along the way. The achievement of the NSSG is separated into two phases: 2000-15, and 2015-30. Yet even before looking at the broader picture, the EU has to decide and define the role of the proposed European Rapid Reaction Force, designed to put around 60,000 troops into the field for up to a year. It has to explain and prepare the public for a more pro-active EU peacekeeping/peacemaking role, which will have consequences in terms of resources and possibly serious casualties. The report also argues that the ERRF should be made available for UN peacekeeping operations, inside or outside Europe.

Apart from defining a new military doctrine, the EU will also have to do more to develop its conflict prevention and peacekeeping/peacemaking capabilities, which should place equal (or more) weight on the human and civil aspects of security. Hence the recommendation for the creation of an EU rapid reaction humanitarian agency (RRHA), and the need for a enlarged notion of security defined in military and human terms.

UK government thinking on some aspects of these developments is more advanced than others. However, the consequences for defence procurement at the national and European levels and for the structure of the British and European defence industries have not been fully thought through. The government has no industrial strategy to support the defence industrial base, or the increasingly vulnerable small and medium-sized enterprises (SMEs) in the supply chain. In an industry with significant levels of employment, that oversight may have serious consequences as the impact of overseas outsourcing, defence consolidation and globalisation bites.

The role and performance of the Regional Development Agencies (RDAs) to date has been somewhat underwhelming. The lack of a coherent regional policy does not help. However, this report shows how the RDAs could develop a far more pro-active role in supporting SMEs in the supply chain, and the defence and aerospace high-value sector. The report also makes recommendations to open up the US defence market, and improve the accessibility of the European market. However it stops short of examining the general issue of arms export controls, which would require a separate report. Suffice it to say that adherence to the EU's 1998 Code of Conduct for the arms trade is taken as a sine qua non, and the report's author hopes that the Government shortly finds the time to introduce further legislation in this field, particularly to improve parliamentary scrutiny and regulate arms brokering and trafficking.

On the procurement side, the Government's Smart Procurement initiative should be given a 10,000 mile service to check all is working as intended, although some early results are positive. The MoD and DTI, together with the DETR, should embark upon an industrial and regional impact assessment of any major UK government defence procurement decisions (over £100 million). With increasing defence consolidation, the report argues that the emphasis for future procurement should not necessarily be on cost competition, but on capability and value for money. Certainly, as the report outlines, the role of the Defence Diversification Agency should be boosted, and an Innovation Fund (at a cost of £10 million) created.

While NATO will remain the main focus of the collective defence effort for years to come, the EU will increasingly develop the capacity for autonomous action. The report posits that the US military presence on the continent, which is already at a third of its Cold War level, will reduce by a further half to 50,000 or less (including the Sixth Fleet). By 2030, Russia and the Ukraine would be candidates to join NATO. The report envisages a European Strategic Defence Review (ESDR), a European Combined Joint Staff College (ECJSC), and an EU-NATO Consultation Council. Within the EU, other reforms would include boosting the role and status of the High Representative (currently Javier Solana) and the European Council and creating a Defence Council.

The New Strategic Security Goal for Europe would mean that by 2015, whilst NATO remains the cornerstone of European defence in all-out war, the EU will be capable of carrying out peacekeeping/peacemaking operations, within or outside the EU. In addition, by 2030, the EU will also have developed the capabilities to mount a common defence in the face of any threat to European security. Increasingly, whilst not creating a European army, EU multinational force packages will be the order of the day.

There is, however, a catch for New Labour and the Centre-Left in Europe. If Centre-Left governments want to develop and enhance Europe's defence capabilities, making their armed forces a 'force for good in the world' in more effective peacekeeping/peacemaking operations, this has to be paid for. The report recommends the EU 15 spend a minimum two per cent of GDP should on defence up to 2030, and no less than a third of their national defence budgets on procurement and R&D. Without this spending, the report shows the EU's defence aspirations will become, as the US warns, empty rhetoric. If the EU does manage to spend at these levels (politically difficult in Sweden and Germany for example) for this length of time, it will involve difficult trade-offs with spending on the welfare state and other social priorities. Even Britain, which announced its first real increase in defence spending in a decade in the 2000 Spending Review, and is comfortably within the GDP and R&D and procurement target levels, may find the going hard given its other spending commitments.

Summary of recommendations
Taking a lead in enhancing European defence capabilities

The EU Member States should ensure that a military doctrine is agreed, based upon the Petersberg tasks, as a guide to the purpose, operations and objectives of the European Rapid Reaction Force (ERRF) proposed at Helsinki. This military doctrine should be made public, so that the role of the ERRF is publicly understood and unambiguous.

For planning purposes, EU Member States should commit up to 180,000 personnel to the proposed ERRF. In addition, the EU should put in place a mechanism to annually monitor and review EU Member States fulfilment of the Headline and capability goals outlined at Helsinki and the Capability Commitment Conference.

The EU's Committee for civilian aspects of crisis management, established by the Portuguese Presidency, should have at its disposal a full database of police and civilian experts (regularly updated for rapid deployment), such as infrastructure re-construction experts. This would help provide the EU with a non-military response to crises, in co-operation with the interim Situation Centre/Crisis Cell. The EU should develop a central register of experts willing and able to take part in post-conflict re-construction. The co-ordinating mechanism established by the Council Secretariat should lead this work.

The EU should establish a rapid reaction humanitarian force, able to provide humanitarian and other resources at overnight notice. The European Commission should create a rapid reaction humanitarian agency (RRHA), to co-ordinate conflict prevention activities, and to assist with civilian peacekeeping activities, including policing, humanitarian aid, and reconstruction. Where EU peacekeeping/peacemaking operations are embarked upon, the RRHA should liaise with the European Union's High Representative for the CFSP, and the Military and Political and Security Committees.

Civilian, military-civilian and military tasks lists need to be drawn up as part of the development of a holistic security doctrine, to conduct fully integrated Peace Support Operations (PSOs).

The Kosovo crisis underlined the importance of interoperability between Alliance forces. NATO standard should remain the basis for all interoperability and standardisation doctrine, including for EU-led operations. Forces should be better integrated through a more effective command and control policy and agreement is required on procedures for policy implementation.

Focusing on capabilities

EU Member States should agree a defence spending target of two per cent of GDP, to be implemented at the latest by 2004. Once achieved, no EU Member State should reduce its defence spending below 2 per cent of GDP until 2030, when the target could be reviewed. This target should also be applied to states seeking EU accession.

EU Member States should agree to spend no less than a third of their national defence budgets on R&D and procurement, to be implemented by 2004 at the latest.

The EU should use the European Commission's R&D Sixth Framework Programme (2002-2006) as a vehicle to co-ordinate R&D investment in major areas across the European Union, including the aerospace sector.

The EU should launch a Revolution in Business Affairs (RBA) initiative, to complement the Revolution in Military Affairs (RMA), so that defence ministries and governments emulate best practice in the commercial sector, including the use of commercial techniques, cost management, outsourcing, leasing of equipment, focused logistics, equitable risk-sharing, and long-term partnership agreements between governments and suppliers.

Consolidation, globalisation and transatlantic relations

European tank manufacturers should consider a joint venture to produce the next generation of main battle tank (MBT), when in 20-30 years time the existing generation are obsolete and need replacing. EU Member States should agree joint procurement requirement s for the next generation battle tank, with France, Germany and Britain at the core of a joint programme, managed either by OCCAR or the European Armaments Agency.

As a matter of urgency, the Government, working with the industry, trade unions, MoD and DTI should establish a framework document providing a strategic focus for rationalising and consolidating the shipbuilding industry over the next 15 years (up to 2015).

The US has to do more if it is serious about opening up the US defence market. The US needs to relax its proxy board requirements for FOCI (Foreign Ownership, Control or Influence) firms, and develop the more widespread use of 'special security agreements', similar to the one agreed with Rolls-Royce over Allison. The latter agreements would only be reached with countries and companies qualified for ITAR (International Traffic in Arms Regulations) exemption, particularly regarding export controls, industrial security, intelligence sharing, law enforcement and market access.

There needs to be a move to more 'process based' licensing in the US. There should be a shift away from individual transactions towards certification of internal control procedures, and a complete overhaul of the export licensing system, focusing on procedural implementation rather than licence 'paper chasing.'

The current US National Disclosure Policy (NDP) should be improved through, for example, blanket exemptions in the case of a security agreement between two countries. Another reform could be to establish a government-industry consultation and appeal process.

The ITAR waiver agreed between the US and Canada, should be applied to the UK and other eligible countries as soon as possible, particularly European NATO members. In addition, there should be a stronger partnership between US law enforcement agencies, customs, defence and intelligence agencies in the field of defence-related exports. Instead of relying on a licence to trigger an interagency review, the agencies should collaborate in advance to identify potentially suspect transactions and to notify companies to be on their guard for specific purchase requests from suspect buyers.

The proposed Presidential Commission on the future of the US aerospace industry should be extended to cover transatlantic defence relations, culminating in a European-US summit on the subject.

EU efforts to define a single company law, industrial policy for the aerospace and defence sector and a common European export control regime should be redoubled, but should not discriminate against non-EU firms. OCCAR discussions on defining common defence procurement rules should also take the transatlantic dimension into account.

Procurement issues

The abolition of juste retour is crucial. Juste retour is extremely uncompetitive and inefficient. Establishing a European Armaments Agency by 2003 should be an EU priority. The benefits to the EU of backing an effective EAA, which rejected juste retour, would be significant.

The WEU's WEAG and WEAO should be wound-up over the next three years, and their responsibilities folded into NATO, as the WEU effectively ceases to exist. OCCAR should be retained for the time being and form the model for the operation of the EAA, with the former eventually merging into the latter. EU Member States should only join the EAA when they are able to meet the obligations and responsibilities of OCCAR membership. The end result should be one European armaments agency representing EU Member States, with NATO seeking to achieve wider harmonisation and interoperability between EU and non-EU NATO members, Canada and the United States.

OCCAR should in the meantime be awarded management of further substantial programmes (in addition to the A400M military airbus), to enhance its credibility and status as Europe's leading collaborative armaments organisation, for example Meteor and a future EuroTank project.

The MoD should instigate a study of the effectiveness and the processes adopted in the smart procurement initiative, review progress so far, and consider any changes or improvements which might or might not be necessary. The test for smart procurement will be to secure tangible and demonstrable improvements of project costs, over a measurable period.

As consolidation and globalisation narrows the choice of prime contractor, competition in the UK and elsewhere should be particularly encouraged at the sub-prime level, below the level of the major systems integrators. Competition should be built around the capabilities, competences and processes to deliver a system and maintain it over its life cycle, at the prime level and further down the supply chain. Building on the smart procurement 'whole life' flexible approach, there is need to build-in high performance specifications, upgrades and maintenance costs. This means that the emphasis for future procurement should not necessarily be on initial cost competition, but on capability and value for money over the whole long-term life of the project. Off-the-shelf costs can be deceptive, attractively priced for initial purchase, but with a sting in the tail as maintenance, servicing and upgrade costs are taken into account.

Before the European defence industry can consider participating in joint procurement, there must be political, military and strategic agreement on what is required when by Europe's armed forces. There is a need to agree on a strategic framework for the EU's new defence capabilities, and how they can meet the requirements of deployability and sustainability within the overall force structure. Exact equipment needs will have to be quantified on a multilateral basis, allowing for the principle of interoperability, both amongst the EU Member States and their non-EU NATO allies.

The revision of armaments programmes in the years ahead can provide EU Member States with an opportunity to initiate a process of convergence between EU military doctrines. EU Member States must discuss their defence doctrines with one another, with a view to establishing the broad lines on which the defence sector could develop the military equipment needed for the missions identified. The Petersberg tasks provide a starting point.

Military doctrines must be explored in further depth, as they are the framework in which the European defence sector operates. It is axiomatic that a strong European defence industry is necessary for an effective EU Common European Security and Defence Policy, and to strengthen the existing CFSP. A European defence technology base is also an obvious pre-requisite for a European Security and Defence Identity within NATO.

Defence diversification, industrial strategy and innovation in the UK and regions

UK prime contractors should be encouraged to second staff to work in the Defence Diversification Agency (DDA), especially on supply chain and innovation issues.

An Innovation Fund should be established to support the supply chain and SMEs in the defence sector. An Innovation Fund would give SMEs financial assistance both to pay for new seeding innovation and achieve successful technological transfers. The Innovation Fund would provide a mechanism to assist technological transfer from the defence to the civil sector, and vice versa.

The Government should provide the DDA with £10 million seed money for the Innovation Fund, which in partnership with financial institutions, could lead to an

Innovation Fund worth an estimated £500 million. The DTI should ring-fence some of its innovation funding for the DDA. Such an Innovation Fund would act as a real driving force for defence diversification, giving substance to the DDA's aspiration of becoming 'a world class technology innovation brokerage service to implement Government policy on defence diversification.'

The Government should think about how to co-ordinate better the work of innovation across the DTI, MoD (DERA/DDA), the DETR and the Cabinet Office's Performance and Innovation unit.

The DTI, working with the MoD, the DETR and the Cabinet Office, should draw up a framework strategy document on current and proposed future policies and programmes to support the UK defence industrial base, and the supply chain network. The DTI and MoD should also consider the means of funding more demonstrators in the defence industry, so supporting early development programmes.

The RDAs should recognise the contribution of defence prime contractors to the overall health of regionally located supply chains. Working with Government Offices in the regions and local authorities, the RDAs should draw up strategies to provide support for the sector's larger defence companies, and exercise a stakeholder interest in these core companies. The RDAs should also develop inter-regional approaches to support the defence sector supply chain.

RDAs should adopt transparent and nationally accessible policies towards training and research. RDAs should also recognise that agencies like DERA, the DDA and universities are also vital national assets, and adopt strategies that reflect national and local priorities. RDAs should encourage the development of a single, coherent business support system within the region, so simplifying access and improving cost effectiveness.

RDAs should create single points of contact for information on European business issues and helping with funding applications. RDAs should also improve access to high level educational and training agencies. They could also help the defence industry and supply chain companies (especially SMEs) through the encouragement of single point research and training agencies.

RDAs should encourage the expansion or creation of regional trade associations or comparable bodies. Regional groups of this nature are often best placed to understand the needs of local firms, especially defence sector SMEs and supply companies.

RDAs located in regions of defence industry clusters should ensure that at least one member of the RDA's board has experience of the defence sector and its supply chain.

The MoD should, together with the DTI and DETR, embark upon an industrial and regional impact assessment of any major UK government defence procurement decision. A major defence procurement programme impact assessment should therefore be undertaken by a special cross-departmental body, comprising officials from the MoD, DTI and DETR, with support research specialists as required.

Initially, major defence procurement programme impact assessments would only occur in cases where the value of the contract exceeds £100 million, but this figure should be kept under review.

A new strategic goal for Europe

The EU, when approaching the issue of European defence, must embrace an enlarged notion of security which is defined in military and human terms. More emphasis should be placed on the role of foreign and development policy in security. In UK domestic terms, there should be a more holistic approach to security policy, with 'joined-up' policy co-ordination between the Foreign Office, MoD and the Department for International Development (DFID),

The importance of policy coherence between the Common Foreign and Security Policy (CFSP) and development policy should not be underestimated. In order to achieve a more meaningful definition of security, it is important to stress the necessity of ensuring coherence across First and Second pillar activities (that is broader Community actions/policy and the CFSP). Apart from the military aspects of security, the EU should also focus on the achievement of human security development issues.

A more coherent approach is required across all EU activities, and those of the 15 Member States. One way to help to develop this would be through the introduction of conflict impact assessments carried out by the Policy Planning and Early Warning Unit (PPU) established by the Amsterdam Treaty. The PPU could assess how EU foreign, development, trade, military and arms export policies are impacting on vulnerable countries. This would ensure that the EU, and its 15 Member States, avoid pursuing conflicting policies that only serve to exacerbate tensions and fuel instability.

NATO will remain the main focus of the collective defence effort for Europe in the years ahead, as well as the focal point for transatlantic security co-operation

The institutional relationship between the Council's High Representative and the Commissioner for External Affairs (currently Chris Patten), who also speaks on the CFSP, is not working. The two roles overlap and duplicate each other. With the evolution of the Council as the dominant EU institution, the role of the High Representative and the Council should be paramount.

The High Representative should be the primary international spokesperson for the CFSP and CESDP on behalf of the EU institutions. The High Representative's status should be boosted by being made permanent chair of the Political and Security Committee, and also chair of the General Affairs Council (which brings together EU foreign ministers).

The rotating presidency, which confuses those outside the EU and adversely affects policy continuity, should also be abolished. The EU Commissioner for External Affairs and his/her directorate should act in an advisory role to the High Representative, acting rather like a Permanent Secretary in the British civil service, preparing options and implementing agreed Council policy on the CFSP.

The role of the Council itself should enhanced with regard to the CFSP and CESDP, with the secretariat under the High Representative and Secretary General of the Council preparing a draft annual agenda (to be ratified by the European Council).

In addition to the General Affairs Council, a separate Defence Council should be established, to which EU defence ministers would be invited to discuss CESDP issues. The High Representative could also chair the Defence Council. Other Council sessions (such as the Agricultural Council) would be chaired by a Minister elected by their peers for an annual fixed term.

European Council sessions would be prepared by an expanded Council Secretariat, working on an agreed annual agenda, but chaired on a rotating basis. The European Council, bringing together all the Heads of Government, should be the body which sets the political and economic agenda for Europe. However, the Commission would retain the power of initiative, bringing proposals to the European Council to implement the agreed annual agenda, which the latter could then discuss, amend and ratify.

The EU needs to establish a New Strategic Security Goal (NSSG) which looks beyond the Headline Goal set at the Helsinki Summit. The EU must decide now what its security goals are for the medium to long-term, beyond 2003.

The public should also be informed about the EU's purpose in seeking to establish a CESDP (the 'end game'). The NSSG should fulfil three criteria: political legitimacy, military capability and affordability. By 2015, EU forces (including the European Rapid Reaction Force) should able to carry out a Kosovo-type operation without recourse to US military assets.

EU-NATO relations and institutional links also need to be established on a sound footing. Instead of the current ad hoc arrangements, an EU-NATO Consultation Council should be created. The Consultation Council would form an operational institutional link between the Council, Commission and NATO.

DSACEUR, NATO's Deputy Supreme Allied Commander (who is always a European) responsible for the European Rapid Reaction Force, must sit on the EU's Military Committee as of right, and be invited to Council meetings of EU foreign and defence ministers which discuss the CESDP. Double-hatting of military representatives to NATO and the EU should be agreed standard practice.

The EU should embark upon a long-term study on likely requirements within a 15 year and 30 year planning cycle, including sources of supply, specifications and funding.

Over the period 2000-2015, the EU would gradually increase its operational effectiveness so that by 2015 the European Union would be capable of almost all collective security missions. The progressive expansion of EU tasks and missions would be accompanied by increasing professionalisation of European forces, and the creation of larger pools of highly-trained and well-equipped troops.

By 2015, the EU would be able to provide substantial force packages for peacekeeping/peacemaking operations, within or outside the EU. However, already by 2003, the EU should make available the ERRF, or elements of the rapid reaction force, for peacekeeping/peacemaking operations either in or outside the EU, under UN or other auspices.

Reform of the UN's role in peacekeeping and conflict prevention will be vital in ensuring that the EU can collectively and effectively participate in United Nations' peacekeeping operations. If the UK government's offer to establish the UN military staff college is accepted, the staff college should also offer training and courses in peacekeeping/peacemaking to European military personnel, with particular emphasis on the Petersberg tasks.

To complement the UK's UN peacekeeping initiative and the proposed UN military staff college, a new peacekeeping doctrine for all EU forces is needed. The integration of national elements into a European multinational force raises a number of specific issues, such as doctrine, command language, joint training, objectives, acceptable levels of risk, attitudes to local populations, rules of engagement and the use of force.

A European Combined Joint Staff College (ECJSC), building on the Eurocorps experience, would be a useful mechanism for addressing these issues. The ECJSC should be established by 2003 to plan for EU Peace Support Operations (PSOs), and to work on issues surrounding the role of the European Rapid Reaction Force in support of Petersberg tasks. The ECJSC should complement, and not duplicate the work of the UN military staff college, with the latter concentrating on the broader issues of UN peacekeeping operations.

The EU needs to undertake a European Strategic Defence Review (ESDR), to be completed by 2003. This would define the missions, structures capabilities and resources needed for European forces and act as the core planning framework. After 2003, the missions of EU military forces should be broadened and military tasks increased, so that progressively more ambitious operations can be undertaken. The expansion of missions and tasks will be linked to the progressive professionalisation of European armed forces. The ESDR should be repeated every three years, to match missions with tasks.

The ESDR could also act as a focal point for a public information campaign, to reinforce popular support for developments in EU defence. The UK's 1998 SDR could serve as a model, combining public consultation with a broad dissemination of information. As part of the ESDR, a Europe-wide study should be undertaken to look at the implications of the Revolution in Military Affairs (RMA) for European forces, the possible advantages of RMA, specific programmes and likely costs.

At the heart of European defence planning should be a European Combined Joint Task Force, that is an EU Permanent Military Headquarters onto which European national forces can 'bolt-on'. In addition to EU duties, the Headquarters would co-ordinate operational planning and act as the operations planning link with NATO.

Building on the WEU audit of 1999, the EU needs to establish specific command, control, communications and computer systems for autonomous operations, based on a study of existing assets, planned assets and shortfalls.

Further satellite intelligence capabilities are required in addition to the two Helios 1 satellites (owned by France, Italy and Spain) and designated military satellite communication systems, to avoid dependence on the United States. However, as these satellites are so expensive, and EU Member States may not be able to afford them and meet their strategic capability goals, the EU should examine what further use can be made of the improving Commercial Satellite Imagery (CSI) for Peace Support Operations (PSOs).

The WEU's Satellite Centre at Torrejon in Spain should be transferred to the EU, and it should develop its capacity to analyse photographs from commercial satellites.

The EU should also develop autonomous capabilities in the field of aerial reconnaissance, which is a less expensive option than developing satellites. The EU should pool their UAV programmes to create an autonomous capability, providing battlefield intelligence to its forces.

On the intelligence front, the EU should also establish an EU-level Joint Intelligence Committee (EJIC), along the lines of the UK's JIC, made of senior intelligence figures from each member state. The European Joint Intelligence Committee should share intelligence with the US and NATO, on a reciprocal basis.

In addition to the planned enhancement of a strategic lift capability, the EU should create a European air transport command (Eurolift), as proposed at the Helsinki European Council. Such a command, involving joint logistics, training and maintenance, would improve military efficiency and provide cost savings. Eurolift could also be extended to sea transport and an air-to-air refuelling force.

The 1948 Modified Brussels Treaty and the Article 5 collective defence guarantee it includes for full members should remain, but should continue to be met through NATO, where each nation has a complimentary commitment.

The expertise of the WEU Institute for Security Studies should not be lost. The WEU Institute should be converted into an EU Institute for Security Studies. The EU Institute for Security Studies would become a centre supporting the command and planning elements of the EU, with academic and policy expertise.

The demise of the WEU Assembly means a level of democratic accountability will have disappeared. A second chamber of the European Parliament (or senate), consisting of national parliamentarians nominated from the EU Member States, associate members, partners and observers of the former WEU could take on the role of the old Assembly. The new senate, or second chamber of the European Parliament should be established by 2002 Only parliamentarians from existing EU member States would have full voting rights, all the others should attend as speaking but non-voting observers. The senate would ensure parliamentary accountability over the CESDP. On appropriate occasions, observers from the Russian Federation and the Ukraine should also be invited to by the

President or Senate Speaker to sessions on the CESDP (to speak but not vote). It is important that the European Parliament's senate does not exclude those countries which previously had rights to attend the WEU, and debate and report on European security issues. The senate should have its own secretariat, building on the strengths of the WEU Assembly administration.

The European Parliament should not become more bureaucratic, however, costing the taxpayers of Europe even more money. With the creation of a senate of 200 national MPs including observers, the ceiling for the number of MEPs in the first chamber should be cut to 500, from a current total of 626. The 500 MEPs in the first chamber should include MEPs from the 13 applicant states, with the figure being revised on the successful accession of the 13th new Member State. This will require a reduction in national MEP quotas at the time of the accession of the first wave of new EU Member States (possibly in 2004), but will save the European taxpayers money.

National MPs in the senate should be paid national parliamentary delegation rates for attendance at the European Parliament, in line with current WEU Assembly payments. The overall effect of the proposed reforms should be a net saving to the European taxpayer. These savings would be higher if France could be persuaded to shift the parliament permanently from Strasbourg to Brussels, instead of parliamentarians commuting between the two institutions (at an additional cost of £100 million per annum).

The EU's new Strategic Security Goal will have two phases, covering from 2000-2015, and from 2015 to 2030. Phase two would see a move away from purely collective security and force projection towards collective defence and ultimately common defence. Over a 30-year planning framework, the EU should undertake work to examine the force levels necessary to protect the European home base from every type of threat, and fight a Major Theatre War (MTW). These developments would suggest a move away from task-sharing in the medium to long-term towards specialisation (especially in logistics), and the emergence of common supranational 'groupements' that replace national units such as regiments and divisions.

It is thus necessary for the EU to move from a combined and joint approach to the establishment of common force packages and elements. This would not mean the creation of a European standing army, but multinational force packages. Planning would have to begin almost immediately, as much military equipment has a thirty to 40-year life-span.

To avoid the marginalisation and isolation of the Russian Federation and the Ukraine, both these countries should be candidates to join NATO by 2030. NATO should invite the Russian Federation and the Ukraine to join its Membership Action Plan (MAP), building on the Partnership for Peace (PfP) initiative, with a view to being full candidates for NATO membership by 2030.

Whilst NATO remains the cornerstone of European defence in all-out war, by 2015 the EU will be capable of carrying out Petersberg task peacekeeping and peacemaking operations on the continent and beyond. In addition, by 2030, the EU will also have developed the capabilities to mount a common defence in the face of any threat to European security.

I: Taking a lead in enhancing European defence capabilities

European defence – the background

In 1999 the US devoted 3.2 per cent of GDP to defence, against 2.2 per cent by NATO's European allies. European NATO countries collectively possess only about 10 per cent of the US capacity to deploy and sustain troops outside the NATO area. *Operation Allied Force* in Kosovo highlighted the Europeans' C4ISR (command, control, communications, computers, intelligence, surveillance and reconnaissance) capability gap. The Europeans also lacked air and sea transport and logistical support. The EU jointly failed to match even half the US's capabilities in the fields of strategic lift, strategic intelligence or command and control. (See, for example, House of Commons, 2000)

Table 1.1 Defence expenditure as a percentage of GDP 1999

Belgium	1.5%	Netherlands	1.8%
Czech Republic	2.2%	Norway	2.2%
Denmark	1.6%	Poland	2.2%
France	2.8%	Portugal	2.2%
Germany	1.5%	Spain	1.4%
Greece	4.9%	Turkey	5.7%
Hungary	1.6%	UK	2.8%
Italy	2.0%	Canada	1.2%
Luxembourg	0.9%	USA	3.2%

Source: House of Commons (2000)

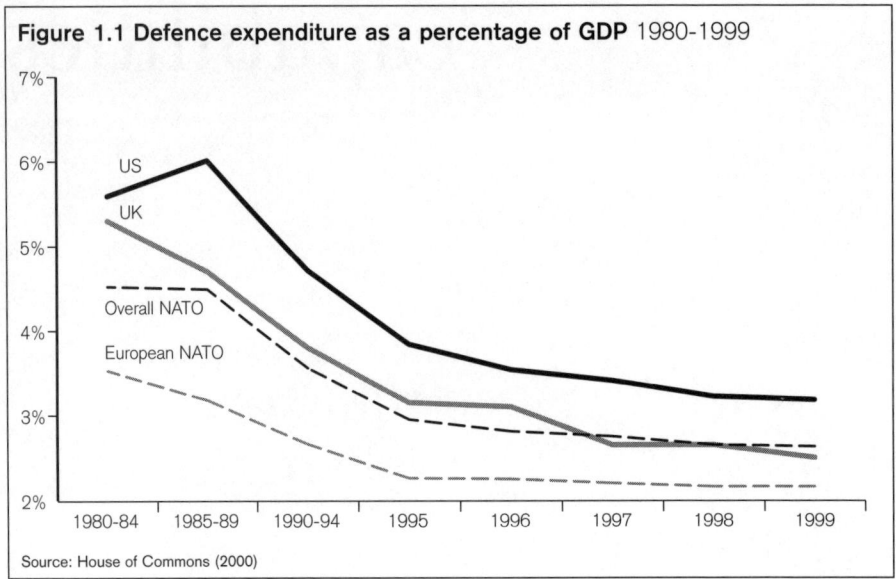

Figure 1.1 Defence expenditure as a percentage of GDP 1980-1999

Source: House of Commons (2000)

During the air war over Kosovo, 85 per cent of the munitions delivered by NATO were American, while only 20 per cent of the strike sorties were carried out by European aircraft (despite Europe having 6,000 fast jets). NATO air forces carried out nearly 10,000 bombing missions during the 78-day air campaign. The US provided over 70 per cent of the aircraft, while the remainder came from 12 countries (Belgium, Canada, Denmark, France, Germany, Italy, the Netherlands, Norway, Portugal, Spain, Turkey and the UK). France flew about 10 per cent of the sorties and Britain five per cent. European aircraft were incapable of carrying out missions in bad weather, and had to be escorted by US aircraft. The Europeans were especially dependent on the Americans for battle control, refuelling, jamming and destroying Serbian radar. The British, with their submarine-launched missile capability, were the only other country apart from the US to launch cruise missiles during the campaign. The US fired 240 sea-launched Tomahawk Land-Attack Missiles (TLAM), the UK 20. The Americans also fired 60 air-launched cruise missiles (ALCM). (See figures in International Institute for Strategic Studies (1999) pp 30-31)

Kosovo showed the Americans had better C4ISR than the Europeans, more accurate precision-guided weapons, better air and sealift resources and logistics, and had greatly improved their capacity to communicate amongst their services. While the US had markedly improved their ability to handle communications and information technology in high intensity warfare since the Gulf war, their European allies had been marking time.

Of the 35 satellites position over Kosovo during the conflict to gather intelligence, just two were European (the Europeans have five in total, the US 65). Consequently, most of the intelligence was supplied by the US. Of the communications capability in the theatre of operations, 90 per cent was American. European force projection capabilities included only two leased roll-on, roll-off sealift ships, compared to 12 RO-ROs for the US, and no fast sealift capability (compared to 8 for the US). The Americans also had 254 aircraft available for large airlift, compared to none for the Europeans. An initial US evaluation noted that the capability gaps: 'were real and had the effect of impeding our ability to operate at optimal effectiveness with our NATO allies'(Adams, 2000).

British Army communications (using the outdated Clansman system) were insecure and overheard by the Serbs. Spares were also in short supply, and about a third were not working during the crisis. Part of the problem lay with the notorious delay in the development and procurement of the still undelivered Bowman radio, a project which had been running since the 1980s. A hard-hitting report from the UK's National Audit Office, released on 5 June 2000, also pointed to other British military shortcomings exposed by Kosovo. In addition to the insecure communications, more than half the missiles carried by the Royal Navy's Harriers were unserviceable within two months due to heat and vibration problems, while nearly half the Harriers relied on spares 'robbed' from other aircraft. A quarter of all precision bombing missions by British aircraft had to be aborted because of bad weather, and had the weather been better there was a real risk of running out of smart bombs, the national audit office claimed. There was also a critical shortage of skilled airmen, with the Royal Signals a reported 23 per cent under strength, and shortages of medical and logistics staff.

When the time came to deploy NATO's peace-keeping force Europe struggled to provide 40,000 troops, even though this was one- fiftieth of its armed forces. As UK Defence Secretary Geoff Hoon said in a speech on 28 March 2000:

> We were forced to rely heavily on American military power to give credibility to the diplomatic campaign. We were stretched to put together a contribution to KFOR. We were not pulling our weight. (International Institute for Strategic Studies, 2000, p16)

Kosovo reinforced the growing opinion in Europe and the United States that the EU had to do more to develop an effective military capability, able to meet the new security challenges facing the continent in the 21st century and give real meaning to the embryonic Common Foreign and Security Policy (CFSP). The CFSP, enshrined in Maastricht and deepened in the Amsterdam Treaty, outlined the putative role of the EU Member States in Petersberg tasks comprising 'humanitarian and rescue tasks, peace-keeping tasks and tasks of combat forces in crisis management, including peace-making.' The Petersberg tasks themselves envisaged a more proactive security role for the EU, with the potential for engagement in conflict prevention or peacemaking in regional crises (as experienced in the Balkans). The reality of Kosovo, however, exposed the gap between aspiration and capability. (See Article J.7.2, Treaty of Amsterdam)

The Petersberg tasks themselves were formulated at the WEU (Western European Union) Ministerial meeting, held at the Petersberg Hotel at Konigswinter near Bonn in 1992. Originally defined as appropriate missions for the WEU in the context of the European pillar of NATO, the Brussels Alliance Summit in January 1994 announced that NATO was ready to support the strengthening of the European pillar of the Alliance by making NATO assets available for WEU operations 'undertaken by the European Allies in pursuit of their Common Foreign and Security Policy.' (House of Commons, 2000)

The WEU, established in 1948 with the Treaty of Brussels, despite a capable administration and engaged Parliamentary Assembly, never showed either the capacity or the political will to decide to take action on the big security issues facing Europe. Signed on 17 March 1948, the Brussels Treaty provided for collective self-defence and collaboration in economic, social and cultural matters. Military/security actions have been mainly limited to a police action in Mostar, the WEU's Multinational Police

Element in Albania (MAPE), patrolling sanctions on the Danube and the Adriatic, and some minesweeping in the Persian Gulf and the Red sea, together with some other military exercises (such as CRISEX 98) and the first joint WEU-NATO exercise, CMX/CRISEX 2000. The lack of political will amongst the 10 WEU full members (UK, France, Germany, Italy, Belgium, Greece, Luxembourg, the Netherlands, Portugal and Spain) and the absence of an operational capability or fully-fledged command structure for the Western European Union explains the organisation's failure to undertake peacekeeping or peacemaking operations (Petersberg tasks) in former Yugoslavia. WEU Member States have instead, perhaps understandably, preferred to turn to NATO in times or crisis, or as in operation ALBA in Albania, relied on ad hoc coalitions of the willing. The WEU is distrusted as inexperienced, and lacking NATO's organisational and military clout (House of Commons 2000).

The initiative to boost EU defence capability was essentially British, although it was pushing at an open door following the European experience in Kosovo. Tony Blair raised the issue of a European common defence policy at the informal EU summit at Portschach, on 24-25 October 1998, as envisaged in Article J.4 (Maastricht) and J.7 (Amsterdam Treaty). Article J.7.1. of the Treaty on European Union (signed on 2 October 1997) states:

> The common foreign and security policy shall include all questions relating to the security of the Union, including the progressive framing of a common defence policy...which might lead to a common defence, should the European Council so decide. European Union, Treaty of Amsterdam, Article J.7.1]

Prime Minister Tony Blair led the debate, which discussed options such as strengthening the European Security and Defence Identity (ESDI) within NATO; merging the WEU with the EU; dividing the WEU between the EU and NATO; and strengthening the EU's role with the WEU still acting as the link between the EU and NATO. It was stressed that none of these options were mutually exclusive, the priority being to have sufficient political will to take action where necessary, backed by an effective European military capability (with NATO remaining the foundation of collective security). Europe, it was suggested at the summit, needed the capacity to act decisively, without the full engagement of the US if so required (Private information supplied to the author).

In November 1998, for the first time ever, the Austrian Presidency of the EU invited the Defence Ministers of the EU to an informal Council in Vienna (3-4 November 1998). No substantive statements were issued, but Finland proposed organising a EU/WEU seminar about Petersberg peacekeeping/peacemaking tasks during the Finnish EU/WEU Presidency in the second half of 1999. Not for the first time (or the last) Britain firmly ruled-out the creation of a European standing army.

George Robertson also told fellow defence ministers that the EU must reform both its military forces and the decision-making process controlling them. Progress continued and gathered momentum with the joint declaration on European defence issued by Prime Minister Blair and President Chirac on 4 December 1998 in St Malo. With both countries' Defence Ministers in attendance to sign the Franco-British military cooperation agreements, the St Malo declaration stated:

> It will be important to achieve full and rapid implementation of the Amsterdam provisions of the CFSP. This includes the responsibility of the European Council to decide on the progressive framing of a common defence policy in the framework of the CFSP. The Council must be able to take decisions on an intergovernmental basis...
>
> To this end, the Union must have the capacity for autonomous action, backed by credible military forces, the means to decide to use them and a readiness to do so, in order to respond to international crises (European Parliament 1998).

The radical element in the St Malo Franco-British declaration was the agreement to develop the capacity for *autonomous* military action, with or without the support of NATO. This element of the declaration was always more enthusiastically promoted in Paris than London (where action with NATO was always preferred), but nevertheless became a cornerstone of the EU's evolving defence initiative.

The St Malo text called for the rapid implementation of the Amsterdam Treaty, and made it clear that the Atlantic Alliance remained the 'foundation of the collective defence of its members.' Europeans would operate within the institutional framework of the EU (European Council, General Affairs Council and meetings of Defence Ministers). The different situation of non-NATO EU countries would be respected. In order for the EU to take decisions and approve military action where NATO as a whole was not engaged, the EU 'must be given appropriate structures' and a capacity for relevant strategic planning, without unnecessary duplication, taking into account the existing assets of the Western European Union (WEU) and the evolution of relations with the EU. The EU would therefore need to have recourse to 'suitable military means' (that is European capabilities pre-designated within NATO's European pillar or national or multinational European means outside the NATO framework) (European Parliament 1998).

The United States signed up to the St Malo principles at the Washington NATO summit on 23-25 April 1999 (WSC 1999a). NATO's 19 countries (including new members Hungary, Poland and the Czech Republic) agreed that they were ready to 'adopt the necessary arrangements for access by the European Union to the collective assets and capabilities of the alliance, for operations in which the alliance as a whole is not engaged militarily as an alliance.' The Washington summit built upon the earlier decision of the Berlin North Atlantic Council of June 1996, which had agreed to develop the European Security and Defence Identity (ESDI) and the concept of the Combined Joint Task Forces (CJTF). The CJTF were designed to provide the WEU with the capacity to undertake Petersberg tasks. The idea was to provide NATO military assets ('separable but not separate' forces) for use by the WEU, to undertake Petersberg tasks such as peacekeeping, peacemaking and humanitarian operations. The role of the WEU in undertaking such tasks at the behest of the EU, with NATO's consent, was enshrined in the Amsterdam Treaty (Article J.7).

The Washington NATO summit emphasised the shift towards enhancing EU military capability, rather than developing the role of the WEU. The summit agreed NATO's Council would provide assured EU access to NATO planning capabilities for European operations, and the presumption of availability of pre-identified NATO resources and common assets for use in EU-led operations. This 'assured access' to NATO capabilities and assets was later challenged by Turkey and Norway, which feared being excluded by NATO's EU member states from decisions and operations affecting European security. It also became clear that the 'presumption of availability' of NATO military assets for EU use would depend on agreement and consensus amongst NATO's 19 members, including the non-EU European member states. NATO's new 'Strategic Concept', agreed by the heads of state and government in Washington, stated the Atlantic Alliance would:

> assist the European allies to act by themselves as required through the readiness of the Alliance, on a case-by-case basis and by consensus, to make its assets and capabilities available for operations in which the Alliance is not engaged militarily under the political control and strategic direction either of the WEU or as otherwise agreed...

However, NATO's much-vaunted 'New Strategic Concept' was a disappointment (WSC 1999b). Repetitive, unoriginal and badly drafted, it did little more than recognise that Russia was no longer a Cold War adversary.

The Atlantic Alliance also agreed that a range of European command options for EU-led operations would be identified, further developing the role of NATO's DSACEUR (Deputy Supreme Allied Commander in Europe, who is always a European), who would be responsible for running EU-led operations. NATO's defence planning systems would also be adapted to improve the availability of forces for EU-led operations. The Washington summit welcomed the new impetus given to the strengthening of a common policy on security and defence by the Amsterdam Treaty and confirmed the stronger European role would help to contribute to the vitality of the Alliance in the 21st century. The NATO summit furthermore stressed that the development of the CFSP, as called for in the Amsterdam Treaty, would be compatible with the common security and defence policy established within the framework of the Washington Treaty. This process, it was asserted, would lead to more complementarity, co-operation and synergy (WSC 1999a).

At the Cologne European Council (3-4 June 1999), six weeks later, EU leaders agreed to work towards:

> the inclusion of those functions of the WEU which will be necessary for the EU to fulfil its new responsibilities in the area of the Petersberg tasks. In this regard, our aim is to take the necessary decisions by the end of the year 2000. In that event, the WEU as an organisation would have completed its purpose.

EU leaders adopted a report by the German Presidency on the 'Strengthening of the common European policy on security and defence'. (European Council Cologne, 1999)

The German Presidency proposed ensuring 'political control and strategic direction of EU-led Petersberg operations so that the EU can decide and conduct such operations effectively.' Furthermore, it was agreed that the EU would need a capacity for analysis of situations, sources of intelligence, and a capability for relevant strategic planning. It was suggested that this might require regular (or *ad hoc*) meetings of the General Affairs Council, as appropriate, including Defence Ministers. A permanent body in Brussels (the Political and Security Committee) consisting of representatives with political and military expertise would be established, together with an EU Military Committee consisting of Military Representatives making recommendations to the Political and Security Committee. An EU Military Staff including a Situation Centre would be created, together with other resources such as a Satellite Centre and Institute for Security Studies. The interim Political and Security Committee (PSC), European Military Committee (EMC) and European Military Staff (EMS) came into being on 1 March 2000.

As regards other military capabilities, it was agreed that Member States needed to develop further forces (including headquarters) that are suited also to crisis management operations, without any unnecessary duplication. The main characteristics were seen to include deployability, sustainability, interoperability, flexibility and mobility. For the effective implementation of EU-led operations the EU would have to determine, according to the requirements of the case, which type of operations to conduct. This could comprise EU-led operations using NATO assets and capabilities, or alternatively EU-led operations without recourse to NATO assets and capabilities.

It was stressed that the Atlantic Alliance remained the foundation of the collective defence of its Members, although the 'different status of Member States with regard to collective defence guarantees would not be affected.' In other words, the EU's non-NATO members would not be required to sign up to article V or 5 of the WEU or NATO treaties, both of which oblige the signatories to defend each other from attack. Furthermore, the Cologne summit agreed to consider satisfactory arrangements for:

> European NATO members who are not EU Member States to ensure the fullest possible involvement in EU-led operations, building on existing consultation arrangements within the WEU. This would include looking at the possibility for WEU Associate Partners to be involved in such operations.

The Cologne European Council took another step towards strengthening the EU's Common Foreign and Security Policy by appointing Javier Solana (former NATO Secretary-General) as the first 'High Representative' combined with the post of secretary-general of the Council. Solana would have to work with the EU Commissioners responsible for external relations, together with the new NATO Secretary-General (appointed in August 1999), former UK Defence Secretary George Robertson. From 25 November 1999, Solana was also appointed Secretary-General of the WEU, succeeding Jose Cutileiro, effectively linking the WEU and the EU (European Council Cologne, 1999).

Prime Minister Tony Blair has laid stress on boosting military capabilities to give credibility to the European defence initiative. April's NATO summit agreed to a 'Defence Capabilities Initiative'(DCI), while the Franco-German summit in Toulouse at the end of May 1999 stressed that Europe should acquire the necessary means to cope with crises. The DCI was NATO's response to the capability gap exposed by Kosovo, and before that Bosnia and the Gulf War. The DCI was aimed at improving Alliance capabilities, especially in the areas of rapid deployment, sustainability, survivability, force projection, command and control and information systems. Increased attention was to be paid to: 'the challenges posed by the accelerating pace of technological change and the different speeds at which the Allies introduced advanced capabilities' (NATO, 1999a).

On the multilateral front, the Western European Union conducted an audit of European military capabilities. The Cologne summit reinforced these trends. Tony Blair gave the process another push at the Anglo-Italian bilateral summit in London in July 1999.

Alongside calls from Prime Ministers Tony Blair and Massimo D'Alema for greater integration of the European defence industry, both leaders unveiled a proposal on 20 July to 'set criteria for improved and strengthened capabilities.' The plan outlined setting 'European-wide goals for enhanced military capabilities' and 'national capability objectives' to achieve these aims. The two leaders said they hoped that the idea would be discussed by the EU and WEU before the end of the year. Lord Robertson, newly-appointed Secretary-General of NATO, told a New Statesman conference on 8 September 1999 that the lesson of Kosovo was clear:

> Europe should do better. This is why we have focused the European defence debate on capability. Capability to decide, and capability to act... We also launched a little-noticed initiative at the British-Italian Summit in July, in which we proposed the development of European defence capability criteria. We want to establish performance goals, both on a collective European basis and on an individual national basis.

George Robertson felt these were early days, and that 'we have much work to do to establish which targets will most readily lead to improvements in capability. We think that we should focus on measuring our performance against the criteria of deployability and sustainability' But he acknowledged there may also be merit in measuring the volume of defence budgets spent on equipment or the level of training that Service personnel receive. It was also felt that what was needed was a package, with some criteria resonating more in some nations than others. In any event, Robertson was looking for progress on all this work by the end of the year. (This speech, given at the New Statesman Conference, 8 September 1999 was also discussed in the editorial, 'Converging on common defence', *Financial Times* 20 July 1999.)

The European Council in Helsinki (10-11 December 1999) started the ball rolling in earnest, with the agreement to establish a European Rapid Reaction Force of 50,000-60,000 by 2003, and with Member States tasked to 'develop rapidly collective capability goals in the fields of command and control, intelligence and strategic transport', including the formation of a European air transport command. The same capability shortfalls had been highlighted by a WEU audit presented to the Luxembourg Ministerial meeting in November 1999. The General Affairs Council was asked to 'elaborate the headline capability goals', while the Helsinki Council called for 'further progress in the harmonisation of military requirements and the planning and procurement of arms.' The European Council adopted two Presidency progress reports on developing the Union's military and non-military crisis management capability, as part of a strengthened common European policy on security and defence.

Helsinki emphasised the need to elaborate the capabilities required to undertake the Petersberg tasks, with or without NATO:

> More effective European capabilities will be developed on the basis of the existing national, bi-national and multinational capabilities, which will be assembled for EU-led crisis management operations carried with or without recourse to NATO assets or capabilities.

Particular attention would be devoted to the capabilities necessary to ensure effective performance in crisis management: deployability, sustainability, interoperability, flexibility, mobility, survivability and command and control, taking account of the results of the WEU audit of assets and capabilities and their implications for EU-led operations.

The Helsinki proposals referred to the 'Common European Security and Defence Policy' (CESDP), also sometimes referred to as the ESDP. The CESDP was in fact the title of the European Defence Initiative launched by Tony Blair at the informal European Council at Portschach in Austria in October 1998. The CESDP had its roots in the Maastricht Treaty's reference to the possibility of 'common defence' in 1991. Maastricht committed EU Member States to 'define and implement a common foreign and security policy' (Article J.1), including the 'eventual framing of a common defence policy, which might in time lead to a common defence.' The CESDP is distinct from the European Security and Defence Identity (ESDI), which is a NATO initiative designed to develop the 'European pillar' of the Atlantic Alliance, including the European nations' use of NATO assets and capabilities in crisis management operations. There is however, an obvious overlap between the development of the CESDP and the ESDI, both of which are intended to strengthen European defence capabilities and hence the 'European pillar' of NATO (European Council, Helsinki 1999a, Annexes I-IV; European Council, Helsinki 1999b; House of Commons 2000).

Helsinki underlined the EU's determination to develop an autonomous capacity to take decisions, and where NATO as a whole was not engaged, to launch and conduct EU-led military operations in response to international crises. The EU's leaders agreed that the process 'would avoid unnecessary duplication and does not imply the creation of a European army.' Interestingly, given the debate about the right of intervention in another country during a humanitarian crisis, the European Council recognised the primary responsibility of the UN Security Council for the maintenance of international peace and security.

On what has been dubbed the European Rapid Reaction Force (ERRF), the EU agreed that:

> Co-operating voluntarily in EU-led operations, Member States must be able, by 2003, to deploy within 60 days and sustain for at least 1 year military forces of up to 50,000-60,000 persons capable of the full range of Petersberg tasks. (European Council Helsinki, 1999a, Annexes I-IV)

There has been some discussion of whether this in fact means that the military requirement is for a force of some 180,000 military personnel, given the need for force rotation. However, it is apparent that the requirement to maintain a force of up to 60,000 in the field for up to a year, as stated at Helsinki, would mean that the overall Rapid Reaction Force would have to be at least three times the force deployed in the conflict zone. Senior military figures in NATO are unequivocal, as General Sir Rupert Smith, Deputy Allied Supreme Commander NATO (DSACEUR) indicated when he addressed the ESDI seminar in Portugal on 6 April 2000:

> In addition, and on the basis that individuals are deployed for 6 months at a time, Sustainability means that in order to maintain our Headline Goal of 60,000, we need about 180,000 troops; one lot on operations, one lot coming off operations and the next lot getting ready to go. In practice and based on experience I contend that by the time some have left the armed services, are ill, or promoted and so on, it will be more than this; the factor is nearer 4:1.

Of course not all 60,000 might be needed, and the force might be able to be sustained from within the 60,000, but this would not be providing the maximum European rapid reaction force envisaged at Helsinki.

In a way, in agreeing the Headline Goal of a European rapid reaction force of 50-60,000, the EU was putting the cart before the horse. Instead of picking an arbitrary figure of a Corps-level force, a more logical way to proceed would be for the EU Member States to agree exactly what the force would be used for, the various military-political scenarios, the likely intensity of operations, an agreed military doctrine and only then embark upon an examination of the military capabilities required to meet the objectives set. Instead, at Helsinki, the heads of government agreed the overall level of forces required (up to 60,000), and left the question of objectives (military, operational and political), to another time. It is the task of the Capability Commitment Conference in November 2000 (previously referred to as the Capability Pledging Conference) to ensure that the EU Member States commit the necessary forces to make the ERRF a reality by 2003. It is obvious that further work needs to be done on the ERRF framework, and it is essential that a military doctrine be agreed between the EU Member States, based on the Petersberg tasks, as a guide to the purpose, operations and objectives of the rapid reaction force. These should also be made public, so that the role of the ERRF is publicly understood and unambiguous. In addition, the EU should put in place a mechanism to annually monitor and review EU Member States fulfilment of the Headline and capability goals outlined at Helsinki and the Capability Commitment Conference.

As General Sir Rupert Smith, DSACEUR said at the ESDI seminar, when referred to the rapid reaction force:

My final principle is a Common Way or Doctrine – for the employment of these forces. In particular, we need a Common Way in the complex circumstances of these operations we have been conducting recently, where the objectives are not the simple ones associated with the defence of the nation state.

There is a reason why the EU Member States proceeded to establish the ERRF before working out the modalities of exactly what it was for, what it would be capable of doing, and how it should operate. The Europeans felt under pressure to address the capability gap exposed in Kosovo, and were anxious to avoid being bogged down in arguments on institutional and operational minutiae. Time and again, the British Government said what mattered was enhancing Europe's defence capabilities; institutional matters could wait. The priority, therefore, was to establish a credible plan of action to enhance the EU's military capabilities, and its ability to decide and act effectively.

Helsinki also tasked the incoming Portuguese Presidency with continuing the work of the Finnish Presidency, including conflict prevention and establishing a committee for civilian crisis management. The focus on crisis management is significant. The EU made it clear that its priority was to establish the necessary capabilities to deal with military and non-military crises. There was no intention or attempt to create a military capability to provide collective or territorial defence for EU Member States. What was being proposed was strictly limited in ambition and scope. The aim was for the EU member States to 'assume their responsibilities across the full range of conflict prevention and crisis management tasks defined in the EU Treaty, the Petersberg tasks.'

In this connection, the objective was for the EU to have an autonomous capacity to take decisions, and where NATO as a whole was not engaged, 'to launch and then to conduct EU-led military operations in response to international crises.' In order to assume these responsibilities, the EU also agreed that it had to make more effective use of civilian crisis management resources, creating a 'rapid reaction capability.' The intention was therefore to create a balance between military and non-military crisis management capabilities (European Council, Helsinki, 1999, see Annex IV)

The UK House of Commons Defence Select Committee was keen to establish the point that the EU security initiative was limited to 'crisis management', a fact the British Ministry of Defence was happy to emphasise. Geoff Hoon, the UK Secretary of State for Defence, told the House of Commons Defence Select Committee in February 2000:

> whilst NATO must remain the cornerstone of our security and defence policy the European Union should be given the capability to decide to act

militarily in support of its Common Foreign and Security Policy. Not, I emphasise, for collective defence but for crisis management where the Alliance, as a whole, is not engaged... I would emphasise that collective defence remains the responsibility , through Article 5, of NATO' (House of Commons 2000a)

Article 5 of the NATO Washington Treaty, states:

an armed attack against one or more of [the Allies] shall be considered an attack against them all and...if such an armed attack occurs each of them...will assist the Party or parties so attacked by taking...such action as it deems necessary, including the use of armed force.

The UK Government further stated (27 June 2000), in response to the Defence Select Committee's report on 'European Security and Defence' that:

The Committee rightly recognises that the European security and defence arrangements currently under development are for crisis management, not for collective defence. The Committee recommends that that in the public debate about European defence, this distinction should be made clear. The Government agrees. We must be clear that we are not building structures to rival NATO; indeed as the Committee acknowledges, the Government firmly believes that strengthening European capability will strengthen the Alliance as a whole. In the Alliance context, improved capabilities will be available both for crisis management and for collective defence, as required. (Government Observations on HOC 2000a, 13 July 2000)

The European Council at Santa Maria da Feira in Portugal (19-20 June 2000) proved another milestone in the European Union's long march towards a Common European Security and Defence Policy (CESDP). Building upon the initiative launched at Cologne and reinforced in Helsinki, the EU agreed at Feira to develop a military and civilian crisis management capability, including both the European Rapid Reaction Force and 5,000 police officers for international missions. By 2003, EU Member States agreed to provide up to 5,000 police officers for international missions across the range of conflict prevention and crisis management operations. EU states also agreed to identify and deploy, within 30 days, up to 1,000 police officers. EU guidelines would be produced for international policing.

The EU's agreement to invite European member states of NATO that were not EU members, (such as Turkey and Norway) to participate in EU-led operations, together with non-members of NATO like Russia and the Ukraine, was an important signal that the European Union wished its defence initiative to be as inclusive as possible. It also hoped to head-off any splits within NATO between EU and non-EU members, while reassuring the USA that there would be no de-coupling of the Atlantic Alliance. Similarly, it was hoped that this gesture of inclusiveness would allay fears in Moscow that the EU's defence initiative could be aimed against Russia's historic and strategic interests in Europe.

The Portuguese Presidency also succeeded in establishing a 'Committee for civilian aspects of crisis management', which first met in June 2000. A co-ordinating mechanism was set up by the Council Secretariat, with the priority objective of establishing a database on civilian police capabilities in the EU. This would help provide the EU with a non-military response to crises, in co-operation with the interim Situation Centre/Crisis Cell established by Javier Solana as Secretary General of the Council and High Representative for the Common Foreign and Security Policy (CFSP).

The EU's Committee for civilian aspects of crisis management, established by the Portuguese Presidency, should have at its disposal a full database of police and civilian experts (regularly updated for rapid deployment), such as infrastructure reconstruction experts. This would help provide the EU with a non-military response to crises, in co-operation with the interim Situation Centre/Crisis Cell. The EU should develop a central register of experts willing and able to take part in post-conflict reconstruction. The co-ordinating mechanism established by the Council Secretariat should lead this work.

The EU should establish a rapid reaction humanitarian force, able to provide humanitarian and other resources at overnight notice. The European Commission should create a rapid reaction humanitarian agency (RRHA), to co-ordinate conflict prevention activities, and to assist with civilian peacekeeping activities, including policing, humanitarian aid, and reconstruction. Where EU peacekeeping/peacemaking operations are embarked upon, the RRHA should liaise with the European Union's High Representative for the CFSP, and the Military and Political and Security Committees.

Civilian, military-civilian and military tasks lists need to be drawn up as part of the development of a holistic security doctrine, to conduct fully integrated Peace Support Operations (PSOs).

For the first time, Feira laid down the modalities for developing EU-NATO relations in areas covering security issues, capability goals, the procedures for EU access to NATO assets, and the definition of permanent consultation arrangements. The European Council recommended that the EU 'should propose to NATO the creation of four '*ad hoc* working groups' between the EU and NATO on the issues which have been identified' (European Council, Santa Maria da Feira, 2000, Annexes).

Although a start, it was apparent that co-operation between the EU and NATO had a long way to go, as the arrangements proposed at Feira showed the *ad hoc* nature of the consultation mechanisms between the two organisations. It is surprising, and disconcerting, that even following the Cologne EU summit a year before, very little thought had been given to how there could be effective institutional links and consultation between NATO and the EU as the latter developed the Common European Security and Defence Policy. As one official commented, business breakfasts between Javier Solana and the NATO Secretary-General were hardly going to be sufficient.

The Feira Council also sought to establish permanent political and military structures as soon as possible after the Nice European Council in December 2000, under the French Presidency. These would include the EU's Political and Security Committee and the Military Committee (proposed at Helsinki) and would follow the Capabilities Commitment Conference to be held in November 2000, to ensure the EU Member States pledged the wherewithal for the European Rapid Reaction Force and enhanced capabilities for command and control, intelligence and strategic transport.

US attitudes to European defence

The attitude of the United States to the EU's Common European Security and Defence Policy initiatives have been ambivalent, and sometimes contradictory. America supported the European Security and Defence Identity initiative at the NATO Council in Berlin in 1996, but has not always spoken with one voice on the development of the CESDP within the European Union. The US's problem is that while it wants more effective 'burden-sharing' from the Europeans when it comes to supporting military operations in Europe (and that means more effective European defence capabilities), it is nervous that the CESDP could be a prelude to the de-coupling of the EU Member States from the North Atlantic Alliance. Some politicians in Washington fear the French, in particular, still resent US leadership in NATO and would not be unhappy if the EU eventually detached itself from the Atlantic Alliance. While the old argument about 'burden-sharing' goes back to the 1950s (and has less resonance today), and US suspicion of Paris is long-standing, US worries about de-coupling from NATO and unnecessary duplication of Alliance assets continues to be a cause of concern today in Congress, the Pentagon and the State Department.

The US's ambivalent attitude to the EU's ambitious plans to enhance its defence capabilities has led to some frustration in European capitals. Lord Robertson, former UK Defence Secretary and current NATO Secretary-General, expressed it well when he said:

> There has always been a bit of schizophrenia about America, on the one hand saying 'You Europeans have got to carry more of the burden', and then when the Europeans say 'OK, we'll carry more of the burden', they say 'Well wait a minute, are you trying to tell us to go home?'

Tony Blair was also aware of the dilemma, as he pointed out to the North Atlantic Assembly in November 1998: 'Our US allies have often called for more equal burden-sharing. They have not always been keen to see a greater European identity of view.' (North Atlantic Assembly, forty-fourth annual session, Edinburgh International Conference Centre, Edinburgh, 13 November 1998)

Publicly at least, the US has generally encouraged greater defence co-operation in Europe, with the important caveat that it does not lead to de-coupling, duplication or dissent in NATO. US Secretary of State Madeleine Albright told NATO ministers in December 1998 that the US and Europe should work together to:

> develop a European Security and Defence Identity, or ESDI, within the Alliance, which the United States has strongly endorsed. We enthusiastically support any such measures that enhance European capabilities. The United

States welcomes a more capable European partner, with modern flexible military sources capable of putting out fires in Europe's own back yard and working with us through the Alliance to defend our common interests. The key to a successful initiative is to focus on practical military capabilities. Any initiative must avoid pre-empting Alliance decision making by delinking ESDI from NATO, avoid duplicating efforts, and avoid discriminating against non-EU Members (Truscott P 1999).

Development of the ESDI had been publicly endorsed in the April 1999 Washington Summit, with the 19 NATO members (including of course the US) welcoming '…the further impetus that has been given to strengthening the defence capabilities to enable the European Allies to act more effectively together, thus reinforcing the transatlantic partnership.' The NATO countries acknowledged the resolve of the European Union to have the capacity for autonomous action. 'so that it can take decisions and approve military actions where the Alliance as a whole is not engaged' (NATO 1999a). Madeleine Albright repeated this theme at a ministerial meeting of the North Atlantic Council held in Florence in May 2000: 'As I have made clear at every NATO Ministerial, America supports a stronger, more capable, Europe that is able to act effectively with us or, if need be, without us.'

Nevertheless, caution about where the ESDI might lead, and the broader complaint about 'burden-sharing' was repeated by Strobe Talbott, the US deputy secretary of state, who told a Royal Institute International Affairs Conference on 7 October 1999:

Many Americans are saying: Never again should the United States have to fly the lion's share of the risky missions in a NATO operation and foot by far the biggest bill. Many in my country, notably members of Congress, are concerned that in some future European crisis, a similar preponderance of American manpower, firepower, equipment and resources will neither be politically or militarily sustainable, given the competing commitments that our nation has in the Gulf, on the Korean Peninsula, and elsewhere around the world.

Strobe Talbott went on to underline US schizophrenia on the issue of Europe's initiative to enhance its defence capabilities:

Will it help keep the Alliance together and that means the whole alliance, European and non-European, EU and non-EU? We would not want to see an ESDI that comes into being first within NATO, but then grows out of NATO, and finally grows away from NATO, since that would lead to an ESDI that initially duplicates NATO but could eventually compete with NATO.

Two months later, at the North Atlantic Council meeting on 15 December 1999, Strobe Talbott tried to clarify the US position following the Helsinki summit, insisting that despite his earlier misgivings, Washington was fully behind the European defence initiative:

> There should be no confusion about America's position on the need for a stronger Europe. We are not against; we are not ambivalent; we are not anxious; we are for it. We want to see an Europe that can act effectively on its own... So Helsinki represented, from our perspective, a step – indeed, several steps – in the right direction. We welcome Helsinki's focus on improving European military capabilities, its recognition of NATO's central role in collective defence and crisis management and that the EU can act 'where the Alliance as a whole is not engaged.'

If anyone had been responsible for the view that Washington was lukewarm over the EU's CESDP initiative, it was Strobe Talbott and the Republican-dominated Congress. However, Strobe Talbott's reference in his London speech to America's global commitments highlighted an important disparity between the strategic outlook of the United States and the European Union. Within the EU 15, only the United Kingdom and France retained the ability to project power beyond the European continent, either to protect perceived strategic interests or the legacy of their respective empires. The United States on the other hand, as the world's only remaining superpower, has global strategic interests and a global national security strategy, with the military and economic capability to project significant power worldwide. SUS strategic planning focuses on the requirements of two Major Regional Contingencies (MRC) or Major Theatre Wars (MTW), with the Gulf and Korea utilised for defence planning purposes. The EU Member States, including France and the UK, have neither the interest, political will, or capabilities to project power around the world, and hence lack any global strategy to do so. The UK's Strategic Defence Review (SDR) for example, sought to give Britain the ability either to respond to a major international crisis like the Gulf War or undertake up to two other smaller deployments (such as in Bosnia, and another more substantial deployment), for a limited period, although the MoD explained : 'We would not, however, expect both deployments to involve warfighting or to maintain them simultaneously for longer than six months.' For the UK then, the most demanding mission would be the challenge of conducting two concurrent medium-scale operations, one a relatively short warfighting deployment, the other an enduring non-warfighting operation. The UK, like the rest of the EU, could hardly be accused of having global delusions of grandeur.

The recognition of America's global role and superpower status is also a cause for concern for some in Europe, who fear the US's tendency towards hegemony, or the drift to what the Russians and Chinese (and others) describe as a unipolar world

(Truscott, 1997a). This tendency to unilateralism on the part of the United States has recently been evident in the debate over America's plans (now deferred by President Clinton) to develop a National Missile Defence (NMD) System, despite vocal opposition from France and Germany in the EU, Beijing and Moscow. In Britain, the Foreign Office was known to be less keen on the NMD system than the Ministry of Defence, which itself remained uncommitted. Abroad, Russia in particular stressed that the NMD would be in breach of the 1972 anti-ballistic missile (ABM) treaty, and could lead to a renewed nuclear arms race.

France has been outspoken in putting the case that a separate CESDP is necessary to counter US unilateralist and hegemonic tendencies. Hubert Vedrine, French Foreign Minister, said in the *New York Times*, 7 November 1999:

> Supposing Europeans really do want to become a power. The willingness of the United States to accept with anybody, and particularly with Europe, partnership that is anything but momentary or limited, and to move from unilateralism to multilateralism, remains to be demonstrated. We would like to believe it. This question underlies the whole question of the European common foreign and defence policy. We cannot accept either a politically unipolar world, nor a culturally uniform world, nor the unilateralism of a single hyperpower. And that is why we are fighting for a multipolar, diversified and multilateral world.

Hubert Vedrine's words have been echoed in Moscow and Beijing, which both fear being marginalised in a world dominated by the United States.

US preoccupation with the imbalance between the American and European defence efforts was also apparent during the Presidential election campaign, with the Bush camp making it clear that the Europeans would be expected to raise defence expenditure under a Bush Presidency. Condoleezza Rice, widely tipped as George Bush's choice for national security adviser, criticised the Europeans for a 'near collapse' in military spending in some parts of Europe. Excluding the UK from her criticisms, Ms Rice said that looking at what Europe needed to do to be a force in the region, such as infrastructure, command and control and air support, it was apparent that 'spending is probably going to have to increase. Whilst welcoming the Helsinki initiative, Ms Rice added: 'The greater danger is that European militaries will not do enough, not that they'll do too much.' To a certain extent, the US emphasis on 'burden-sharing' can be overdone. In part it represents a convenient refrain for politicians, and is of less concern to the US military than more important issues like the interoperability of coalition forces in the field.

The European Councils of Cologne, Helsinki and Feira, and the Treaties of Maastricht and Amsterdam chart the development not only of the EU's defence initiative (given a boost at St Malo), but the evolving nature of the security relationship between the European Union and the United States. The clamour for the Europeans to do more (in security terms) in their own backyard had been growing for some time, as Tony Blair acknowledged in 1998:

> Diplomacy works best when backed by the credible threat of force. The maxim applies to Europe too. Europe needs to develop the ability to act alone in circumstances where, for whatever reason, the US is not able or does not wish to participate. Why should US taxpayers and US troops always have to resolve problems on our own doorstep? (North Atlantic Assembly, 44th annual session, 13 November 1999, Speech by PM Tony Blair)

US willingness to pay for European security was not open-ended. The British Prime Minister recognised that there could be circumstances, and a time when 250 million Americans might to refuse to pay in blood and taxes to fight to protect the security interests of 370 million Europeans (or up to 500 million as the EU enlarges to include up to 28 Member States). As Tony Blair wrote in the *New York Times* in November 1998:

> The imperatives that drove defence spending in America during the superpower standoff are gone. If Europe wants the United States to maintain its commitment to Europe, Europe must share more of the burden of defending the West's security interests.

The Prime Minister stressed that Britain was not talking about a European Army, and that NATO would remain the foundation of Europe's territorial defence: 'The military challenges we face are increasingly about crisis prevention, peacemaking and peacekeeping – about humanitarian operations rather than the collective defence of territory.'

Already, since the end of the Cold War, the number of US personnel based in Europe has fallen from 320,000 in 1989 to 97,510 (excluding 14,000 personnel in the US's Mediterranean 6th Fleet (IISS, 1999). The limit currently set by Congress is 100,000. The US, as expressed by Secretary of State Madeleine Albright, remains concerned by the 'Three Ds': No Duplication, No Discrimination and No Decoupling. The US Administration remains implacably opposed to a CESDP which might 'decouple' Europe from the US, 'duplicate' NATO structures and capabilities, or discriminate against non-EU members (such as Turkey and Norway) (Bereuter, 2000). Lord Robertson, NATO Secretary-General, prefers to talk about the 'Three Is': indivisibility of transatlantic security, improvement of European capabilities, and inclusiveness of all European allies in the process. Both the EU Member States and the Americans realised the security relationship between them was changing, but neither side sought separation, let alone divorce.

Conclusions and policy recommendations

- The EU Member States should ensure that a military doctrine is agreed, based upon the Petersberg tasks, as a guide to the purpose, operations and objectives of the European Rapid Reaction Force (ERRF) proposed at Helsinki. This military doctrine should be made public, so that the role of the ERRF is publicly understood and unambiguous.

- For planning purposes, EU Member States should commit up to 180,000 personnel to the proposed ERRF. In addition, the EU should put in place a mechanism to annually monitor and review EU Member States fulfilment of the Headline and capability goals outlined at Helsinki and the Capability Commitment Conference.

- The EU's Committee for civilian aspects of crisis management, established by the Portuguese Presidency, should have at its disposal a full database of police and civilian experts (regularly updated for rapid deployment), such as infrastructure reconstruction experts. This would help provide the EU with a non-military response to crises, in co-operation with the interim Situation Centre/Crisis Cell. The EU should develop a central register of experts willing and able to take part in post-conflict reconstruction. The co-ordinating mechanism established by the Council Secretariat should lead this work.

- The EU should establish a rapid reaction humanitarian force, able to provide humanitarian and other resources at overnight notice. The European Commission should create a rapid reaction humanitarian agency (RRHA), to co-ordinate conflict prevention activities, and to assist with civilian peacekeeping activities, including policing, humanitarian aid, and reconstruction. Where EU peacekeeping/peacemaking operations are embarked upon, the RRHA should liaise with the European Union's High Representative for the CFSP, and the Military and Political and Security Committees.

- Civilian, military-civilian and military tasks lists need to be drawn up as part of the development of a holistic security doctrine, to conduct fully integrated Peace Support Operations (PSOs).

- The Kosovo crisis underlined the importance of interoperability between Alliance forces. NATO standard should remain the basis for all interoperability and standardisation doctrine, including for EU-led operations. Forces should be better integrated through a more effective command and control policy and agreement is required on procedures for policy implementation.

II. Focusing on capabilities

Some early criteria

Europe's comparative weaknesses in the defence field are well-known. Not all of them, such as the existence of separate national defence establishments and the resulting overhead costs, can be overcome without the unlikely creation of a United States of Europe with its own armed forces. However, major inefficiencies are could be avoided. For example, ten years after the end of the Cold War, many European countries still have force structures geared to territorial defence, with massive manpower requirements, designed to repel a land invasion from non-existent Warsaw Pact countries. The EU countries field armed forces of 1.8 million, compared to 1.4 million for the US. Of the European forces, 1.3 million (or two-thirds) are British, French, German and Italian. Many of these soldiers are cheap conscripts, but the bloated force structures and mass armies drain the bulk of limited and relatively shrinking defence budgets. Recently, France, the Netherlands, Spain, Italy and Belgium have decided to end conscription.

Little resources are left for force projection, as illustrated by the examples of Germany, Greece and Italy. Between them, these three countries have standing forces of 800,000 (about 60 per cent of the US total), but they spend only 14.6 per cent of the US total on procurement. In the case of Germany, Berlin spends more than 86 per cent of its defence budget on personnel, infrastructure and support, and only 15.6 per cent on equipment. In 1999, the ten WEU member states spent only half of the American figure on procurement and only a quarter of US expenditure on R&D.

Important as overall levels of expenditure are, of greater significance is the level of expenditure allocated to procurement, R&D, technology, and achieving the aims of deployability, flexibility, mobility, survivability and interoperability.

A collective effort and the political will to foster convergence of EU defence policies is required. Some countries have undertaken initiatives to reorganise their armed forces in the light of the end of the Cold War, with Britain in the forefront with its Strategic Defence Review (SDR). Between 1990 and 1998, largely under the Tory Government, military manpower declined by 32 per cent, RAF aircraft by 30 per cent, tanks by 45 per cent, destroyers and frigates by 27 per cent, and infantry battalions by 27 per cent. UK Defence spending fell from 5.3 per cent of GDP in 1984 to 2.8 per cent in 1997. Similarly, numbers in the Armed Forces fell by a third between 1979 and 1997 (by over 100,000), with the Army having 5,000 less personnel than its trained requirement. By 1997, the UK Armed Forces were suffering from severe 'overstretch, with forces deployed in Northern Ireland, Germany, Belize, Cyprus, Bosnia, the Gulf, the Falklands, Gibraltar, West Africa and the West Indies' (Truscott,1997b).

The UK's 1998 SDR planned to establish Joint Rapid Reaction Forces by 2001, with the command and control, lift and logistics to move two brigade sized forces with air and naval support at short notice. This rapid reaction force was to be backed by the purchase of two additional roll-on, roll-off ships (to improve strategic sealift), the acquisition of four C17 large aircraft or their equivalent, and the consideration of long-term options like the European Future Large Aircraft. A new tanker for air-to-air refuelling would also be considered. The SDR also projected the replacement of three small aircraft carriers with two large aircraft carriers from around 2012, capable of deploying 50 aircraft, giving the Royal Navy greater expeditionary capabilities. On 22 March 2000, UK Defence Secretary Geoff Hoon announced that by 2002, the Joint Rapid Reaction Forces would be able to draw forces from a pool of up to 50 warships and support vessels, four brigades and 260 aircraft. A new Joint Helicopter Command had also been formed. The overall effect was to modernise the British Armed Forces, providing a rapid reaction capability, enhancing force projection, deployability, mobility, survivability and sustainability more suited to the peacemaking/peacekeeping operations likely in the 21st Century.

The SDR made it clear that future British deployments (Sierra Leone notwithstanding) were likely to be in coalition:

> future operations will almost always be multinational. Britain will usually be working as part of a NATO, UN or Western European Union force, or an ad hoc 'coalition of the willing.' This means that we do not need to hold sufficient national capabilities for every eventuality, just as we did not plan to defeat the Warsaw Pact on our own. But it also means that we need balanced, coherent forces which are capable of operating effectively alongside forces from other countries (MoD 2000a).

France has embarked upon a process of reducing its standing forces from 500,000 (mainly conscripts) in 1995 to 350,000 professionals by 2002. Paris planned to abolish conscription by 2003 and create a joint Land Action Force Command for expeditionary operations, rather like the UK SDR's Joint Rapid Reaction Force (planned from 2001). France's 1994 defence white paper recognised that French forces would incapable of autonomous operations and would have to fight in coalitions in the future.

The realisation by both France and Britain that future major operations would be fought in coalition indicated the changing nature of the role of national armed forces. Whereas small-scale operations might still be feasible on a national basis, any significant military operation in the future, including peacemaking/peacekeeping operations, would be undertaken on a multinational level, whether with NATO, the UN, the EU or any combination of a 'coalition of the willing.' The days of independent national warfighting, last seen by the UK in the Falklands and before that in Suez in 1956, were effectively at an end.

Germany has launched its own review of its armed forces, and agreed to participate in NATO deployments outside Germany in 1994. German planning centred on creating a professional inter-service Crisis Reaction Force by 2000, comprising 54,000 troops in six brigades, with 18 air squadrons and three transport wings. The Germans have still not planned major investments in airlift, sealift or advanced munitions and communications. In September 1998, Berlin began a defence review, with an independent Commission on Common Security and the Future of the Bundeswehr. The Commission, headed by former German President Richard von Weizsacker, planned for a cut in the military from 463,000 to 320,000. Military conscription would be kept for just 30,000 draftees, selected by lottery. The army's own general-inspector recommends 399,000 and min-conscription. German plans focus on deployability, airlift resources and a professional Crisis Reaction Force. Ending conscription is particularly difficult in Germany for political reasons, given the unhappy history with purely insulated professional armies. Military service is seen as a tool to bind civilians and the military closer together (Lutz, 2000)

In September 1999, when the Italian Government decided to end conscription and professionalise its armed forces, its defence minister said:

> the total professionalisation of the military instrument is for Italy an important step towards ensuring its role in the new Europe, and enabling it to carry sufficient weight in the European defence and security identity.

The idea of establishing formal 'defence convergence criteria' held some sway in the early discussions on enhancing Europe's defence capabilities. Francois Heisbourg made the case for establishing EU defence convergence criteria in the early summer of 1999, a suggestion which was taken up by the Anglo-Italian summit in July the same year. Prime Ministers Tony Blair and Massimo D'Alema agreed to set criteria for improved and strengthened defence capabilities, national capability objectives and 'European-wide goals' (See Chapter I). However, the enthusiasm for establishing, monitoring and implementing European-wide defence convergence criteria or capability criteria soon dissipated. Instead, the EU Member States shifted emphasis to enhancing Europe's defence capabilities themselves, which was seen as more practical, meaningful and achievable.

Heisbourg's thesis foundered for several reasons. The original idea was that EU Member States could decide, through the European Council, to converge on a set of criteria with the idea of increasing defence force projection capability, and reducing manpower where necessary. A comparison was made with the convergence criteria agreed between the EU Member Sates on the path to the euro and Economic and Monetary Union (EMU). It was argued that, as with the euro, the agreed defence convergence criteria could have a galvanising and mobilising effect on the EU 15. As an example, the share of procurement and R&D expenditure could be raised to the same level of the UK. Currently the divergence between EU Member States is significant. The UK spends 36.6 per cent of its total defence spending on procurement and R&D, compared to 7.1 per cent for Belgium. The overall level of the armed forces could also be tied to a percentage of the population. The UK, for example, only has 0.3 per cent of the population employed in the armed forces, whereas Greece has 1.5 per cent. Long-term criteria could be accompanied by an immediate commitment not to further reduce defence spending per person. In 1997 France spent the most per head of the population on defence in the EU ($708), whilst Spain spent the least ($196) (Heisbourg, 1999).

Other defence criteria, Francois Heisbourg suggested, could be added, including allotted financial contributions to the creation of a theatre command capability, so that the Europeans could run an independent multinational task force. As well as monitoring the level of procurement and R&D expenditure, account could be taken of the level of training and combat-readiness of armed forces belonging to the EU Member States. Although Heisbourg thought it was 'temping to suggest a rise in defence spending in a number of countries, this would probably be politically unacceptable.' Javier Solana, former Foreign Minister in the Spanish Socialist Cabinet, weighed into the debate on 15 September 1999: 'These convergence criteria should focus less on the money governments put into defence budgets and more on what they get out in terms of flexible forces.' The shift to enhancing military capabilities, rather than establishing broad defence convergence criteria, was underway.

There were real practical problems associated with the 'defence convergence criteria' approach. There was a danger that once set, the defence convergence criteria would have no real meaning and little effect. The result could be a broad set of aspirations, expressing 'wish-lists' across a wide range of issues. Monitoring progress would be problematic, as it would be difficult to set objective enough criteria to allow for accurate measurement and implementation. While it was relatively easy to measure a country's procurement and R&D expenditure, it was more difficult to measure the more difficult areas of deployability and sustainability. Would it in any case be of any use or relevance if Luxembourg's total Armed Forces of 768 personnel were 100 per cent deployable, or Portugal spent 30 per cent of its $1.5 billion 1999 defence budget on R&D and procurement (rather than 25 per cent)? Another difficulty would be monitoring the quality of R&D and procurement spending. It would be necessary to commission a major review study at regular intervals to measure progress towards the defence convergence criteria. Unlike the EMU, there would not be a distinct goal, or club membership to aspire to for successful Member States (they were already in it), with the possibility of exclusion for the unsuccessful or tawdry. There was also the issue of how the defence convergence criteria could be made to work for all 15 EU Member States, with their different traditions, especially the so-called 'neutral' non-

NATO states of Austria, Finland, Sweden and the Republic of Ireland.

In short, broad 'defence convergence criteria' would not work. Instead, the EU decided at Helsinki in December 1999 to concentrate on practical defence capabilities, epitomised by the agreement to the Headline Goal of a rapid reaction force of some 50,000-60,000 troops by 2003. Other collective capability goals would be devised, covering command and control, intelligence and strategic transport. The emphasis was firmly on the capabilities 'output' of what the EU member states could do collectively to enhance their security. This led in turn to agreement to hold a Capability Commitment Conference in November 2000, where each EU Member State would commit forces and the wherewithal to achieve the Headline and collective capability goals.

Yet despite the move away from setting universal defence convergence criteria, there is a strong case for setting two important standards or criteria which should be met by all EU Member States, if they truly wish to enhance their defence capabilities. This is because while slimming-down armed forces and creating professional, well-equipped armies will save money compared to the old Cold War variant of massive armies of conscripts, it will not be enough.

The UK has recognised that even with a re-structured military (and the introduction of 'smart procurement'), the new commitment to rapidly deployable, well-equipped modern forces will cost extra money. This was accepted by the UK Treasury, which allocated the first real increase in the MoD defence budget in a decade in the July 2000 Spending Review. In 1999, UK defence spending stood at 2.6 per cent of GDP. The fact that spending was raised at all was a recognition by the Blair Government that the new commitments on European defence, if the EU was serious about them, would cost extra money. Britain could also hardly claim to be leading the initiative on enhancing Europe's defence capabilities if it cut defence spending in real terms, or allowed spending to remain static. However, spending will continue to decline as a proportion of GDP.

The first criteria which should be agreed is that no EU Member State should reduce its defence spending to below two per cent of GDP. This target should be agreed up to the year 2030, given the long lead-in time for new technology and procurement projects. This would be a useful benchmark in showing the EU's commitment to enhancing its defence capabilities, especially vis-à-vis the United States, and give the European Union the collective resources to get on with the job. Defence expenditure below the 2 per cent GDP level will not enable the EU to collectively meet its defence commitments. On the grounds of equity, it is also unjust that while certain EU Member States meet their defence commitments, others conspicuously fail to do so. If EU Member States do not put their money where their mouths are, they should cease their rhetoric about strengthening the Common Foreign and Security Policy (CFSP), the Common European Security and Defence Policy(CESDP) and the European

Security and Defence Identity (ESDI) within NATO. There can be no real CFSP, and no common defence policy, let alone a common defence of the EU, without paying for it. As Lord Robertson, NATO Secretary-General said in June 2000: 'We are not going to get tomorrow's defence on the cheap.' Lord Robertson made it clear that restructuring the military away from Cold War structures and making them more efficient would free up resources from existing budgets:

> But overall, it the Europeans are going to rise to the challenge of the post-cold war world, then more money will have to be invested. Static and declining defence budgets will make a mockery of the ambition to tackle troublespots before they become a crisis (Nicoll, 2000a)

The two per cent GDP minimum will be difficult, especially for the Centre-Left Governments in Europe. It is always difficult for the Centre-Left to justify spending on defence, rather than schools and hospitals. The signs of the political willingness to spend more on defence in Europe do not look particularly promising, although the picture is patchy. The example of the UK speaks for itself, but figures collated by NATO show that eight members (Belgium, Denmark, Germany, Netherlands, Luxembourg, Spain, Hungary and Canada) are spending less than two per cent of GDP on defence, with five (Italy, Norway, Poland, Portugal and the Czech Republic) just above this level.

The German Social Democrat-Green coalition has pledged to cut defence spending. In the autumn of 1999, the German government announced it would reduce defence spending by DM 18.6 billion over the following four years, an ominous portent for the future of the EU's defence initiative. However, as defence minister Rudolf Scharping admitted to SPD members of the Bundestag, German Armed forces are not capable of serving Europe or NATO in their current state. Scharping's solution is to cut manpower from the current level of 332,800 (including 114,000 conscripts), freeing up money for equipment. The 15.6 per cent of the German defence budget spent on equipment compares to 24.8 for the UK, 18.4 for France and 18.6 per cent for the US. However Gerhard Schroder's government still spends only 1.5 per cent of gross domestic product on defence, which even with the proposed re-structuring, is unlikely to release the resources necessary to transform the German Armed Forces into a mobile, rapidly deployable force equipped with the latest technology for effective peacemaking/peacekeeping tasks (IISS, 1999; House of Commons, 2000)

The spending of the French Socialist government of Lionel Jospin compares favourably with the UK's defence effort. France spends 2.8 per cent of its GDP on defence, with 26.9 per cent of its defence budget devoted to R&D plus procurement (compared to 36.6 for the UK, 32.6 for the US).

Outside NATO but in the EU, Goran Persson's Social Democratic government in Sweden announced swingeing defence cuts in October 1999. The Swedish government announced the axing of 6,500 jobs in defence, laying-off 4,000 officers and 2,500 civilians, and cutting the number of army brigades from thirteen to six, saving around £300 million. The air force was cut from ten to eight divisions, while the navy cut the number of surface ships from 24 to 12. While peacekeeping forces would be doubled from 900 to 1,800, Sweden's contribution to enhancing Europe's defence capabilities would be necessarily negligible. If the eleven Centre-Left parties in government in Europe were to follow Sweden's example, Europe would be confined to a cameo role as US infantry auxilaries in future peacekeeping/peacemaking operations on the continent. (Swedish Ministry of Defence 1999); Vipotnik, 1999).

The second criteria which should be agreed amongst EU Member States is that individual Member States should aim to spend at least a third of their national defence budgets on R&D and procurement. Despite the difficulties of measuring the quality and effectiveness of such spending, there are important reasons to consider establishing R&D and procurement criteria. A major reason is to close the capability gap which has opened up between the Europeans and the US, and to address the issue of the Revolution in Military Affairs (RMA).

The Revolution in Military Affairs (RMA)

The 'Revolution in Military Affairs' (RMA) can be defined as the application of modern information and communications technology to warfare. RMA encompasses three technological advances, which underpinned the USA military and technical superiority in Kosovo's *Operation Allied Force*. The first is intelligence, surveillance and reconnaissance (ISR), and the use of sensors in aircraft, which can be used to develop a complete picture of the battlespace. The second is in command, control , communications and computers (C4), which gather and process data supplied by the sensors. This information can then be converted for use on visual display units, which can be used to select targets for various combat assets (such as tanks, aircraft, missiles). Thirdly, the use of long-range precision strikes, for example using Tomahawk cruise missiles, guided by the Global Positioning System of satellites. The US J-STARS system, an airborne ground-surveillance system, enabled the Americans to display on one screen every vehicle in a 200 kilometre radius (Grant, 1999).

The Europeans generally did not, and still do not have, the range of RMA capabilities being developed by the US. In a way this is not surprising give that the RMA debate began in the United States without any reference to NATO's European allies, and the need for full Atlantic Alliance interoperability. The US was concerned initially with achieving the interoperability of its own four services. *Joint Vision 2010*, the US Joint Chiefs of Staffs' view of the future of warfare, hardly refers to coalition military operations, and focuses on issues like information superiority which would give America's joint forces dominance across the whole range of warfighting situations.

Yet the RMA gap between the US and Europe is not as desperate as some would like to believe. European defence companies are technologically capable of producing RMA type weapon systems. There are only certain areas where Europeans do not possess significant RMA capability, stealth technology being an important example. With advances in commercial technologies such as digital communications and microelectronics, there is now more spin-off from the civilian sector to the defence industry than vice-versa. With increasingly trans-national companies and cross-border joint ventures and partnerships, European-based companies are no less able to exploit RMA technology than companies headquartered in the US.

European countries, led by the UK and France, are in fact developing and acquiring significant RMA-type technology. The UK's SDR referred to exploiting the synergistic combination of long-range precision-strike capabilities with networks of advanced sensors and data processors. This would lead to 'significant improvements in military capabilities.' France, through its 'model army 2015' project, was also focusing on developing RMA technologies. One German commentator on the RMA stated:

No doubt, wars and militaries in the 21st century will be dramatically different from those of today. New services, structures and organizational forms will establish themselves. Units will become smaller, faster, and more manoeuvrable. They will be modular and multi-functional. Independent operations by individual services will become a rarity, if they occur at all. Hierarchies will grow flatter; the number of components existing and networked on one level will increase (Mey, 1998)

Precision strike weapons are already a priority acquisition for both the France and the UK. France has developed the Apache family of air-launched cruise missiles, and are planning to procure 500 Scalp-EG missiles with a range of over 250 kilometres and accuracy to within one metre, plus other Apache derivatives. The missile has an all-weather capability through Global Positioning System (GPS) guidance. European missile company Matra BAe Dynamics (MBD) is developing new versions of the Storm Shadow/Scalp EG cruise missile. In late 1995, the UK announced the purchase of 65 conventionally-armed Tomahawk land attack cruise missiles (TLAM) from the US, to be deployed on its nuclear-powered attack submarines. The latter were used by the British in the Kosovo air campaign. In 1996 Britain's Ministry of Defence (MoD) awarded a £600 million contract for the acquisition of 900 Storm Shadow missiles, the British version of the Scalp. In late 1999, Italy also decided to buy Storm Shadow cruise missiles, while Germany is developing an air-launched cruise missile of its own, the Taurus. Furthermore, in July 2000 Defence Secretary Geoff Hoon announced measures to improve the UK's military shortcomings identified in Kosovo, particularly priority capabilities to launch precision attacks on static, mobile and armoured targets in all weather conditions, and action to improve communications security. The Defence Secretary stated the MoD would develop the Maverick anti-armour missile, enhance security for air-to-air communications, and work to provide the RAF with a precision guided all-weather bombing capability (using Global Satellite technology).

While Britain's Tomahawks arrived in time for Kosovo, France's cruise missile capability was still not ready. The French Defence Ministry's 'lessons learned' document on the Kosovo campaign stated: 'French participation in the air raids was reduced by the absence of equipment whose arrival with the forces is expected in a very short time.'

European countries are already acquiring or developing a range of ISR systems. The UK, France and Germany have significant technological capabilities in the field of reconnaissance drones and observation missiles. France, the UK and Italy also have national airborne ground surveillance programmes. French and German CL-289 UAVs (Unmanned Aerial Vehicles) flew around 200 reconnaissance missions over Serbia, with the British Phoenix UAV also seeing some action. Furthermore, France is deploying the Helios series of optical observation satellites, and is interested in developing new optical and radar observation satellites. The development of medium altitude reconnaissance drones is likely to provide EU countries with all- weather observation capabilities. In the future, a European radar observation satellite could also enhance EU all- weather capabilities.

European countries have several satellite communications systems, including the UK's Skynet 4, French Syracuse, Spanish Hispasat and Italian Sicral. The British are planning a Skynet 5 system, while the Franco-German Bimilsatcom programme will provide global coverage, with the first satellite due to launch in 2005. All the major European countries are now investing in digitised C4 (command, control, communications and computer)systems. The UK plans to introduce a formation-level battlefield management system (FBMS) by 2007, while France has deployed in FBMS in Bosnia since 1995. France is further developing the FELIN soldier system programme which will integrate infantry within a digital battlefield management system, allowing real time information exchanges. The use of commercial-off-the-shelf technologies (COTS) is making digitisation programmes relatively more affordable. The Dutch Army's new Integrated Staff Information System (ISIS) is COTS-based and is one of the most advanced C2 (command and control) systems deployed in NATO. The German Defence Ministry has stated that commercial products can supply 95 per cent of the German armed forces' technology requirements. Over the next 10-15 years, European countries should have developed capabilities for real-time transmission of data and images.

So although there is a distinct 'RMA gap' between Europe and the USA, there is not really a huge 'technology gap.' While the US is ahead in qualitative and quantitative terms, for the purposes of the practical peacemaking/peacekeeping operations that are of most concern to EU Member States, the capabilities that they lack are either being developed or are technologically attainable. The problem is one of scale, resources, and the time-lag between development and acquisition. There is no doubt the Europeans are behind in technological terms, but they are by no means out.

The RMA-type programmes referred to above are almost all based on European technology, complemented in some cases by transatlantic cooperation. European companies are thus perfectly capable of meeting the technological requirements for RMA-type weapons. Only the UK's acquisition of US Tomahawk cruise missiles represented an 'off-the-shelf' purchase of RMA military technology.

NATO's Defence Capabilities Initiative in April 1999 was especially designed to address European shortfalls in key military RMA–type capabilities and force projection. The DCI identified deployability, sustainability, survivability, force projection, command and control and information systems as priority areas. Fifty-eight specific capability initiatives have been launched following the DCI, to help address the shortfalls and address the capability gap between the US and its European allies. However, given the budgetary implications of the capability initiatives, European countries are unlikely to find them all affordable, leading to the need to set achievable priorities. With the exception of C3 (command, control and communications), most European countries will focus on non-RMA acquisition activities, for example developing strategic transport and logistical support (see above, chapter 1).

RMA-type capabilities are not cheap. The cost of a significant RMA suite of capabilities has been estimated at around $15-16 billion. This would include a C4 system to cover three army divisions and three air wings, 50 UAVs, 1,000 cruise missiles, 5,000 short-range precision weapons, 500 advanced air-to-air missiles, a squadron of partially stealthy aircraft, and several batteries of theatre missile defence (TMD) systems. The stealth and TMD capabilities alone would cost $4.5 to $6.5 billion. Such a suite of capabilities is likely to remain unaffordable for some time for EU countries (Grant, 2000).

On economic grounds, it would therefore make sense for European governments to concentrate on the affordable end of the scale, focusing on the development of C4 and precision-strike weapons, as indicated in the 1999 WEU audit of military capabilities (Rapson Report 2000, pp12-13). Less emphasis was placed on sensors, or developing costly reconnaissance and surveillance systems. The WEU audit of military assets and capabilities available to WEU countries was submitted to the meeting of the WEU Council of Ministers in Luxembourg in December 1999. At the meeting, the French Defence Minister summed up the conclusions:

> These conclusions certainly show that, as things currently stand, European capabilities are not wholly negligible: the audit reveals that we have the capacity to deploy 100,000 men, 500 aircraft including 300 fighter planes, and a series of naval assets including a sea-air component and an amphibious component. But at the same time the WEU audit stresses two aspects that we must constantly bear in mind:
> - we need to strengthen the operational capability of our forces (ensuring they can be deployed quickly and operate together over a period of time with the maximum degree of security) in order to gear them to post-cold war crises;
> - we must concentrate on the qualitative aspect of strengthening our capabilities, particularly by making good the shortcomings that exist in the areas of assessment, command and projection which are necessary for the implementation of the whole range of Petersberg missions.

The Minister went on to identify seven generic capabilities that should appear on a check list to strengthen the capabilities of 'defence Europe': strategic situation assessment (including proper intelligence), planning and operational control, deployability in strength, high-intensity combat capacity, sustainability, standardised training procedures and interoperability at all levels. None of these capabilities are beyond the reach of the leading European nations.

Several arguments can be made for the European military to focus on C4 and precision strike.

The disparity in precision-strike capacity was the most obvious manifestation of US technological superiority and European dependence on American military assets. Such dependence on US long-range precision strike capacity will not be politically sustainable in Washington in the long-term, and would seriously hamper any attempt by the Europeans to launch any autonomous attack operation. Interoperable C3 systems are becoming increasingly essential in order to pool sensor data, share a common operational picture and synchronise planning and execution among coalition partners. The ability to rapidly process and communicate a vast amount of information is at the heart of the RMA.

There is thus no reason or need for the European allies (even if they had the political will or money) to replicate the US's global force posture. Some mix of high and lower technology forces will be sufficient to carry out the main operations expected of the European Rapid Reaction Force proposed at Helsinki. These are limited to the Petersberg task peacemaking/peacekeeping role, with a preference for coalition operations including US assets, not full warfighting operations encompassing territorial defence. The latter would in any case engage the whole of NATO under Article 5 of the Washington Treaty, while the stated emphasis of the EU defence initiative is on crisis management operations, rather than engaging in full-scale conflicts. A crucial task will be to determine the exact mix of high and lower technology. For example, relatively low cost UAVs could potentially meet most of Europe's ISR requirements.

Nevertheless, unless there is a clearly focused effort by the EU to focus on a military posture based around force projection and RMA-type capabilities, the Europeans will not able to undertake autonomous crisis management operations or contribute effectively to US-led military operations.

Table 2.1 illustrates the importance of downsizing and professionalising the armed forces, so that budgetary resources are released for R&D and acquisition. This is critical to closing the 'RMA gap' between the European allies and the United States. The US, with an armed forces 1.4 million strong, is able to spend a much higher percentage of its defence budget on R&D and procurement than most EU Member States, who collectively have some 1.8 million in their combined armed forces. Only the fully professionalised British armed forces spend more of their defence budget than the US on R&D and procurement (36.6 to 32.6 per cent), with the UK spending more proportionally on and R&D. France (at nearly 30 per cent) is close behind, and the professionalisation of their armed forces should bring them up to US and British levels. The British and French defence budgets constitute almost half the European NATO total, pushing the latter's R&D and procurement defence spending figure to 26.7 per cent. Defence restructuring by

Germany and Italy, and the introduction of a professionalised armed forces, would bring the European R&D and procurement total close to the US level. This would greatly assist in closing the most glaring aspects of the RMA and capability gap which has opened up between Washington and NATO's EU members. It should, however, be borne in mind that the Europeans have to catch up with almost a decade of high US spending on RMA technologies following the Gulf War.

Table 2.1 1999 Defence spending (1997 US $ million)

	Defence budget $mill	R&D (%)	Equipment (%)	%budget devoted to R&D plus equipment
France	28,353	3,148 (11.1)	5,242 (18.4)	29.6
Germany	23,790	1,262 (5.3)	3,715 (15.6)	20.9
Italy	15,609	298 (1.9)	1,905 (12.2)	14.1
Netherlands	6,797	64 (0.9)	1,380 (20.3)	21.2
Spain	5,464	170 (3.1)	744 (13.6)	16.7
UK	33,254	3,909 (11.8)	8,263 (24.8)	36.6
NATO Europe	135,213	8,946 (6.6)	27,152 (20.1)	26.7
US	252,3793	5,324 (13.9)	47,052 (18.6)	32.6

The above figures do not include the Czech Republic, Hungary or Poland. See: The Military Balance 1999-2000(1999), Oxford: Oxford University Press, table 8, p37]

Source: *The Military Balance, 1999-2000* International Institute for Strategic Studies

Greater synergies in European defence R&D and procurement would also enhance the EU's defence capabilities. France's post-Kosovo assessment noted that 'France could exhaust itself attempting to attain an inaccessible level, or will be forced to abandon entire research areas, if it does not coordinate its investments with its European partners.' (French Defence Ministry, 1999) The EU could use the European Commission's R&D Sixth Framework Programme, which will run from 2002 to 2006, as a vehicle to coordinate R&D investment in major areas across the European Union, including the aerospace sector. The fifth framework programme channelled 15 billion euros into pan-European projects in areas ranging from biotechnology and telecoms to aeronautics.

A great deal of Europe's resources are wasted through redundant fixed assets , infrastructure and duplication of effort in non-essential areas. In addition to a European RMA, a Revolution in Business Affairs (RBA) is required, so that governments and defence ministries emulate best practice from the commercial sector, including the use of commercial technicques, cost management, outsourcing, leasing of equipment, focused logistics, equitable risk-sharing, and long-term partnership agreements between governments and suppliers (Algeri *et al*, 2000, pp 68-70).

Conclusions and policy recommendations

- EU Member States should agree a defence spending target of two per cent of GDP, to be implemented at the latest by 2004. Once achieved, no EU Member State should reduce its defence spending below 2 per cent of GDP until 2030, when the target could be reviewed. This target should also be applied to states seeking EU accession.

- EU Member States should agree to spend no less than a third of their national defence budgets on R&D and procurement, to be implemented by 2004 at the latest.

- The EU should use the European Commission's R&D Sixth Framework Programme (2002-2006) as a vehicle to co-ordinate R&D investment in major areas across the European Union, including the aerospace sector.

- The EU should launch a Revolution in Business Affairs (RBA) initiative, to complement the Revolution in Military Affairs (RMA), so that defence ministries and governments emulate best practice in the commercial sector, including the use of commercial techniques, cost management, outsourcing, leasing of equipment, focused logistics, equitable risk-sharing, and long-term partnership agreements between governments and suppliers.

III.
Consolidation, globalisation and transatlantic relations

Defence consolidation and globalisation

Globalisation can be defined as the integration of the political, economic and cultural activities of geographically and/or nationally separated peoples. Globalisation is not new, but is accelerating due to a range of positive factors such as the information revolution, the end of the Cold War, the spread of capitalism and free trade, rapid global capital flows, the liberalisation of financial markets, international academic and scientific collaboration, and faster and more efficient transportation. Globalisation has been an environmental characteristic of virtually every capital-intensive commercial industry for around a decade, and has more recently spread to the service sector. The impact of globalisation on industry is to broaden markets, the supplier base, and ownership from a national to an international basis. In the post-Cold War era, national captive defence industrial markets no longer exist, with a less defence-intensive industrial base increasingly international in character. This in turn is the result of reductions in defence spending on procurement and R&D on both sides of the Atlantic, the explosion in commercial sector high-tech R&D, acquisition reform and a shift in procurement emphasis from weapons/platforms to the information technologies amplifying their capabilities.

Since 1980-84, European NATO defence spending has fallen from 3.5 per cent of GDP to 2.2 per cent (in 1999), while US spending fell from 5.6 to 3.2 per cent of GDP over the same period (see Figure 1.1 in Chapter 1). US procurement and R&D budgets are down by a hefty 70 per cent and 25 per cent in real terms respectively, since the late 1980s. The traditional core of the defence sector will focus increasingly on the integration of commercially-developed advanced technology to produce military capabilities. Already, the commercial sector is now driving the development of much of the advanced technology integrated into modern information-intensive systems. This is especially true of the consumer microelectronics and software sectors. Military-technological advantage in the future will depend less on advanced component and subsystem technology developed by national defence industries than from defence sector system integration skills, wherever they may be located. Increasingly, defence sector system integration skills will transcend national boundaries, as the defence sector itself becomes more 'globalised' (Cevasco, 2000).

Against the background of globalisation, the defence sectors in the United States and Europe have witnessed unprecedented consolidation and rationalisation since the end of the Cold War. The process of defence sector consolidation began in the United States, with the famous 'last supper' in 1993, when the Defence Secretary Les Aspin encouraged the chiefs of the US defence industry to go away and merge. Many of them obliged, as Figure 3.1 shows.

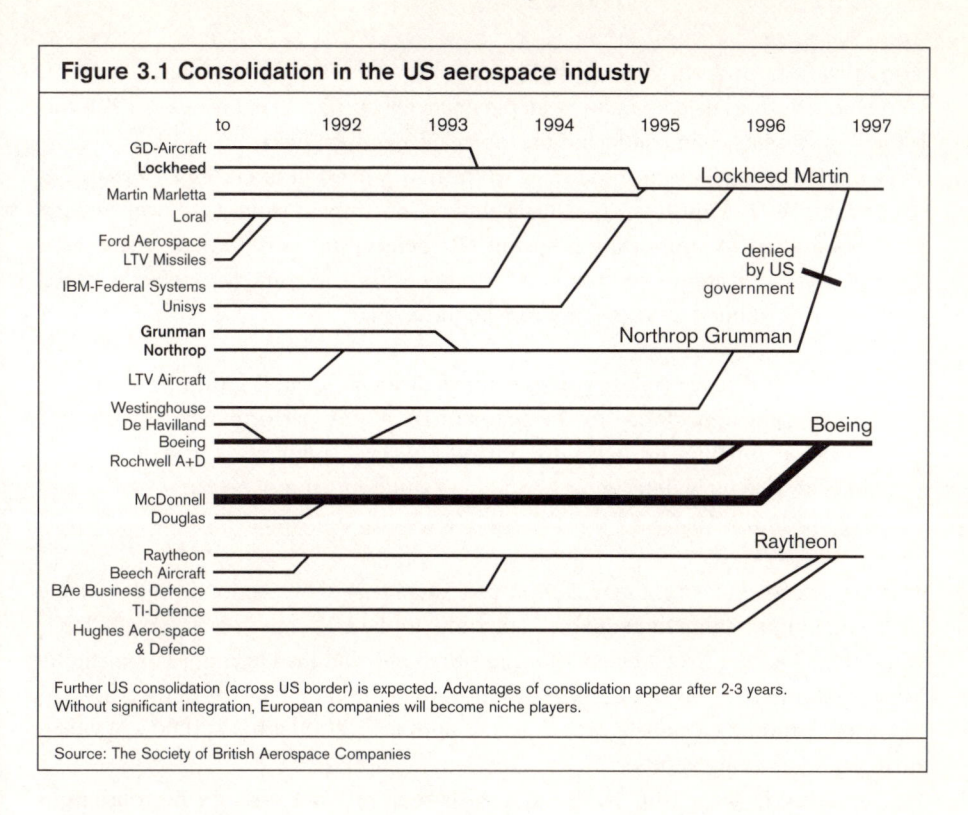

Figure 3.1 Consolidation in the US aerospace industry

```
                    to      1992    1993    1994    1995    1996        1997
        GD-Aircraft ─────────────────────────┐
           Lockheed ─────────────────────────┴──────────── Lockheed Martin
    Martin Marietta ──────────────────────────────────────┘
              Loral ──┐
     Ford Aerospace ──┤                                  denied
       LTV Missiles ──┘                                  by US
  IBM-Federal Systems ─────────────────────────┐         government
             Unisys ──────────────────────────┘
           Grumman ────────────────────────┐
           Northrop ───────────────────────┴──── Northrop Grumman
        LTV Aircraft ──────────────────────┘
      Westinghouse ─────────────────────┐
        De Havilland ───────┐           │
             Boeing ────────┴───────────┴─────────────────── Boeing
        Rochwell A+D ─────────────────────────────────────┘
          McDonnell ═══════════════════════════════════════╝
            Douglas
                                                       Raytheon
           Raytheon ─────────────────┐
      Beech Aircraft ────────────────┤
  BAe Business Defence ──────────────┼──────────────────── Raytheon
         TI-Defence ─────────────────┤
       Hughes Aero-space ────────────┘
          & Defence
```

Further US consolidation (across US border) is expected. Advantages of consolidation appear after 2-3 years. Without significant integration, European companies will become niche players.

Source: The Society of British Aerospace Companies

Systems integrators in the defence aerospace and electronics industries such as General Dynamics, Martin Marietta, McDonnell Douglas, Grumman, Northrop and Hughes were taken-over or merged, leading to the loss of a million US jobs. The consolidation in the US defence industry in the 1990s was driven by declining defence budgets, the cost of new technology and the need to achieve economies of scale to achieve a competitive edge. The decision by the Pentagon in mid-1998 to block Lockheed Martin's acquisition of Northrop Grumman brought to an end this phase of rationalisation, and highlighted the concern to avoid an anti-competitive US defence market.

To put the size of the US defence industry in perspective, in 1996 the collective sales of the eight largest European defence undertakings reached $60 billion. At the same time, the three largest US defence companies had sales exceeding $90 billion. Moreover, American defence exports were increasingly out-competing the European defence sector. In 1985, the EU's imports of military goods manufactured in America were valued at four times its similar products to the US. This had risen to five times higher by 1990, and to six by 1995. The European Commission now estimates hat European governments buy defence goods from the US worth seven times what the Americans buy from Europe. The United States defence sector was becoming more competitive through its process of rationalisation, and was increasingly penetrating the European defence market. Throughout Europe, defence industry employment fell by 13 per cent between 1993 and 1995, as increasing competition and the 'peace dividend' bit hard.

In the UK, British defence spending fell from 5.3 per cent of GDP in 1984 to 2.8 per cent in 1997. However, the New Labour Government came to power in May 1997 committed to supporting a strong UK defence industry, which it saw as a strategic part of Britain's industrial base, as well as the country's defence effort. Furthermore, Labour's 1997 manifesto recognised that:

> the British defence industry is integral to Britain's overall industrial base and of vital importance to the nation's economic performance. British defence companies are recognised as world-class competitors in a sector characterised by high-technology and high value-added processes and skills.
> (Labour Party, 1997)

Britain's defence industry, the manifesto proclaimed, was an 'economic and strategic asset', vital in providing high quality equipment to the UK armed forces. As the UK's Minister for Defence Procurement, Baroness Symons, told the Defence Manufacturers Association on 16 September 1999: 'All of us, whether in the US or Europe need to export our products. The defence industry supports 445,000 jobs, 130,000 of which are dependent upon exports.'

Given the challenge from the US and the end of the Cold War, the response from Europe's leaders was to encourage the rationalisation of Europe's defence industry. Like the Americans, European defence manufacturers were under pressure to rationalise and achieve cost-savings. The European defence sector needed to be able to compete with the US and be globally competitive. In the post-Cold War era, military budgets were being slashed while the cost of research and development rose. Before rationalisation started in earnest in Europe there were 43 major defence-related European companies, compared to just 14 in the US (dominated by the three giant contractors Lockheed Martin, Boeing and Raytheon). The European defence sector was fragmented, with 10 prime contractors for military aircraft and helicopters (compared with five in the US), four for main battle tanks compared with one in the US, 12 for missiles (America has three), and at least 14 for tracked armoured vehicles compared with two in the United States.

The European companies were also chasing a combined European defence budget around half the size of the United States, a situation which was economically unsustainable. In former British Defence Secretary George Robertson's words, the UK defence industry had to 'rationalise or die.' On 9 December 1997, Germany, France and the UK issued a joint statement calling upon the aerospace and defence electronic industries in their respective countries to 'present a clear plan and detailed timetable...for restructuring and integration [of the industry] by 31 March 1998.' The idea was to create a single European Aerospace and Defence Company (EADC), with Sweden, Italy and Spain joining this group in the summer of 1998. However, this vision was later to founder in January 1999, when BAE Systems acquired Marconi, General Electric Company's defence arm.

Following this ambitious target, on 20 April 1998, the Ministers of Defence of Germany, Spain, France, Italy and the UK adopted a Joint Declaration agreeing to seek to harmonise the needs of their armed forces in such a way as to avoid duplication of effort, and to harmonise their acquisitions, research and technological development policies and defence aspects of their export procedures. At the same time, the Ministers acknowledged that it was primarily up to industry to create a rationalised industrial base for European defence, and encouraged the industry to continue its efforts in this respect. On 6 July 1998, the governments of Britain, France, Germany, Italy, Sweden and Spain signed a Letter of Intent (LoI), with the aim of establishing a regulatory and procedural framework to assist the restructuring of the European defence industry. The LoI covered the issues of security of supply, export procedures, security of information, research and technology, harmonisation of military requirements and intellectual property rights (IPR). The idea was to define principles, organisational questions and responsibilities as a prelude to appropriate follow-on arrangements and agreements.

The LoI was eventually followed, two years later, by a Framework Agreement signed by the UK, France, Germany, Italy, Spain and Sweden at the Farnborough Air Show on 27 July 2000. The Treaty was designed to establish practical measures to facilitate the restructuring and operation of the European defence industry, paving the way for more effective defence equipment and industrial co-operation in Europe. The Framework Agreement covered practical and specific measures for improved co-operation on security of supply, export procedures, handling of classified information, treatment of technical information, research and technology and harmonisation of military requirements. Detailed implementation arrangements to broaden and deepen co-operation would be the subject of further negotiation between the six countries.

UK Defence Secretary Geoff Hoon said of the Treaty:

> This is a major development in European defence equipment co-operation. There are clear benefits for each country's defence industry in a Treaty which can help remove obstacles to industrial co-operation and promote improved equipment co-operation in Europe...
>
> Over time, other European countries that share our commitment to the underlying principles of the Treaty will be able to join. This reflects our determination to maintain a strong and competitive base capable of competing with the best in the world (MoD 2000b).

The Treaty sought to create the political and legal framework necessary to facilitate industrial restructuring in order to promote a 'more competitive and robust European technological and industrial base in the global defence market and thus to contribute to the construction of a common European security and defence policy.' Specific proposals included simplifying and reducing export control procedures for transfers and exports of military goods; minimising the use of government-issued end user certificates (in favour of company certificates of use); consultation on the formation of Transnational Defence Companies (TDCs); and pooling information on future Research and Technology (R&T) programmes. The idea was to harmonise R&T programmes and 'establish common defence related R&T programmes where appropriate.' The parties to the agreement would also seek to harmonise their methods of negotiating, funding and letting defence related R&T contracts, with competition the preferred method of placing contracts.

Article 42 of the Treaty referred to the harmonisation of standard provisions appearing in defence contracts, while Article 45 stressed the importance of recognising the need to harmonise military requirements and 'agreeing on the definition of a common concept for force employment and developing a common understanding of the corresponding military capabilities to be implemented.' However, it stopped short of calling for a common military doctrine for the parties to the agreement (let alone the EU), and gave little clue as to how this would be achieved. There was also no reference to the European Rapid Reaction Force agreed at Helsinki, and how this sat with the Framework Agreement, particularly since only six of the EU 15 signed the Treaty. However, the Treaty did call for co-operation in establishing a 'long term master plan that would present a common view of their future operational needs, and a detailed analysis of military capabilities' (Article 46). The six countries also agreed to:

> identify projects that may have the potential for co-operation in the areas of research, development, procurement and logistic support, in order to improve overall military capability, especially in the field of intelligence, Strategic Transport and Command and Control. (Article 47)

The signatories also agreed to look at tasking and funding an organisation with legal personality to manage programmes and proceed to common equipment acquisition, but failed to mention establishing a European Armaments Agency or the *Organisation Conjoint pour Cooperation en la matiere d'Armament* (OCCAR) (Article 48).

The LoI and Framework Agreement mirrored the UK's negotiations with the United States to open-up the American defence market, one of the most highly protected defence markets in the world (the UK defence market is one of the most open). On 5 February 2000, Defence Secretary Geoff Hoon and US Defence

Secretary William Cohen, signed a Declaration of Principles, designed to improve defence equipment and industrial co-operation between the UK and United States. Similar to the LoI and Framework Agreement which followed it, the Declaration of Principles (DoP) was intended to establish principles for improved co-operation on security of supply, market access, exports, handling of classified information, research and technology and military requirements. Under the agreement, UK defence companies doing business in the UK should be treated no less favourably than US defence companies doing business in the UK. Detailed implementation arrangements were the subject of further negotiations between the UK and US defence ministries.

The DoP committed the two defence departments to seek better means to harmonise military requirements, co-operate on R&D, and work on the possibility of 'harmonising procedures for defence materiel acquisition.' On export procedures, the Department of Defense (DoD) and MoD agreed to:

> explore means to achieve greater transparency and efficiency in our national export procedures, in particularly looking to simplify procedures for the export of defence items between ourselves, to establish list of acceptable export destinations...and to pursue measures to harmonise conventional export policies as far as possible.

A high level council was established to pursue these matters.

The Declaration of Principles (DoP), the planned precursor of similar agreements between the US and its allies, was also intended to complement the European Framework Agreement, signed that July at Farnborough. It was symbolic and significant that the US sought an agreement with the UK, before any of its other allies, on closer industrial defence co-operation. This indicated both the closeness of existing industrial defence co-operation, and the degree of political trust between the two governments and defence establishments.

Some 90 per cent of EU defence equipment production is concentrated in five member states: France, the UK, Germany, Italy and Sweden. The UK, Germany, Italy and Spain have worked together on the Eurofighter project (BAE Systems, DASA, Alenia and CASA), while the EH101 helicopter has been developed jointly by the UK and Italy. Joint collaboration projects have also included the Future Large Aircraft (FLA) or Military Airbus A400M involving France, Italy, Britain, Germany and Turkey, Portugal and Spain (involving leading companies such as Aerospatiale, Alenia, BAE Systems , DASA and TAI), and the three-nation GTK/MRAV (multi-role armoured vehicle) armoured vehicle programme. Under the auspices of OCCAR, established in 1996, Germany, France, Italy and the UK have embarked on several collaborative armament projects.

The majority of programmes currently managed by OCCAR are between France and Germany (Tiger combat helicopter, Milan and Hot anti-tank missiles and Roland missiles), some are between France and Italy (such as the FSAF- future anti-aircraft systems family), while others are trilateral. The Cobra anti-radar battery (France/UK/Germany) was OCCAR's first non-exclusively Franco-German programme. There are plans to integrate the third-generation anti-tank missile AC3G-MP (France, Germany, the UK plus the Netherlands and Belgium), the third-generation AC3G-LP anti-tank missile (Germany), and the PAAMS air-defence system (France, Italy and the UK). There are also plans for the integration of the Polyphem missile (France, Germany and Italy), and the Horizon air-defence frigate (France and Germany minus the UK). France, however, dropped out of the GTK/MRAV, leaving Britain and Germany to seek the Netherlands as a replacement partner. OCCAR's record has been mixed, with the International Institute for Strategic Studies stating that development '..has been slowed by continuous disputes over workshare allocations (juste retour)' while long-running programmes like the Tiger helicopter 'are the subjects of tortuous renegotiations and delays.' Certainly, the number of programmes entrusted to OCCAR has been limited, although the four member states have agreed to the A400M being managed by the armaments organisation, despite three of the seven military airbus partners not being in OCCAR (Belgium, Spain and Turkey) (IISS, 1999).

European defence integration and restructuring

European defence integration and restructuring are largely politically-driven processes. Although consolidation would have taken place without the political impetus to create an enhanced European defence capability, the pace and nature of the industrial restructuring which has occurred was heavily influenced and driven by the political dynamics involved. It was Europe's politicians who launched the initiative to enhance the EU's defence capabilities, but they combined that political initiative with the industrial aim of defence consolidation and integration. EU Heads of Government realised that the political objective of a stronger CFSP and CESDP could not be realised without a powerful European industrial defence base, able to close the RMA gap with the US, and provide European forces with modern, up-to-date equipment. European defence consolidation and the EU's defence initiative are therefore inseparable, and are two components of the same drive for EU enhanced defence capabilities.

The UK undermined the goal of greater European defence integration in some eyes both by pulling out of the Horizon frigate project (involving France, Italy and the UK), and by acquiescing in the face of BAE System's purchase of the Marconi defence arm of General Electric Company (GEC). This latter £6.9 ($11.4) billion deal, announced in January 1999, was initially felt to have sabotaged attempts to link up with DaimlerChrysler Aerospace (DASA) of Germany, and reportedly embarrassed and annoyed British Prime Minister Tony Blair, who had promoted European industrial defence consolidation. By creating a British national defence champion with defence sales second only to Lockheed Martin (BAE Systems becoming the world's third largest defence-aerospace group), it was thought the deal would scupper moves towards creating a European Aerospace and Defence Company (EADC). European continental companies would be wary of being swallowed-up in cross-border mergers involving the British defence giant. DASA said the move would 'make balanced European mergers impossible', and that it would create an 'obstacle to future European integration.' (Harnischfeger, 1999)

France had also felt abandoned by the British, as Thomson-CSF and GEC had been attempting to create a Franco-German electronics company. A stumbling block had been the French insistence on an over-valued 50 per cent stake in the business and a demand that the chief executive should always be French. In mid-February the French defence industry took an important step towards consolidation when Aerospatiale merged with Matra Hautes Technologies, the military and space wing of the Lagardere group. The new company was called Aerospatiale-Matra. Seventeen per cent of the shares were floated on the stock market on 5 June 1999. The French government retained 47-48 per cent, Lagardere 33 per cent and Aerospatiale's staff 2-3 per cent. As a result of the merger of Alcatel and Dassault's defence electronics business with Thomson-CSF (in which the French government retains a 34 per cent stake), Thomson-CSF became a major company with 70 per cent of its sales and 30 per cent of its workforce outside France.

Thomson-CSF was determined to go down the cross-border road. It bought Signall in the Netherlands, Thorn Missile Electronics in the Britain, and Shorts Missiles Systems in Northern Ireland. In January 2000, Thomson-CSF put in a cash bid to acquire Racal Electronics, the British defence firm, making the combined firm the second largest prime defence contractor in the UK after BAE Systems. Under the new arrangements, only 32 per cent of the combined workforce would be based in France, with 32 per cent in the Europe and 36 per cent in the rest of the world. The £1.3 billion takeover of Racal increased Thomson-CSF's UK employees from 6,000-15,000, out of a total workforce of 64,500 (see figures on www.thomson-csf.com, www.update.thomson-csf.com, www.racal.com).

Both BAE Systems and DASA remained unhappy at the level of the French Government's stake in the French defence industry, and similar problems dogged the transformation of GIE Airbus Industrie into a genuine European company (and the creation of an Airbus Military Company, responsible for the Airbus A400M). Supported by their governments, British and German industry sought full privatisation of the French defence sector as a guarantee of commercial autonomy. To break the impasse, the British and Germans looked to be negotiating a bilateral solution between BAE Systems and DASA, with the option of the French joining at a later date.

BAE Systems switch from a link-up with DASA to the £7 billion Marconi purchase was not capricious. For several years, Sir Richard Evans, Chairman of BAE Systems, had been pressing for the EADC, or European aerospace and defence company. It was only when a trilateral arrangement with France (given the privatisation issue) was deemed impossible, that BAE Systems and DASA began bilateral negotiations on a merger. However, for a number of reasons the talks did not go well. One of the problems was that although BAE Systems was the larger company, its shares were distributed. DASA's shares were all held by DaimlerChrysler, the industrial giant created by Jurgen Schrempp of DaimlerChrysler Aerospace and Robert Eaton, boss of the US car-maker, Chrysler. DaimlerChrysler therefore wanted to be the biggest shareholder, with a veto over the merged Anglo-German aerospace group. The Germans would therefore have control, and in negotiations continued to haggle about the value of the combined company. Meanwhile, Lord Simpson, managing director of General Electric Company (GEC), who had initially wanted to become part of the BAE Systems-DASA merger, was keen to sell the Marconi defence arm of GEC to the highest bidder. Incidentally. GEC and BAE had discussed merging for about 15 years.

The acquisition of Lockheed Martin's aerospace electronics business (AES), expected to be completed by the end of 2000, will make BAE Systems the largest defence contractor, overtaking its US rival Lockheed Martin. The Lockheed businesses had a turnover of $1.78 billion, operating profits of $118 million and 5,300 employees. The division included Sanders (a specialist in aircraft self-protection systems, tactical surveillance and intelligence systems) with 3,900 employees, and the smaller Fairchild Systems and Space Electronics and Communications. The UK group won the auction against US group Northrop Grumman, with John Weston declaring at the Forum Europe conference in Paris, 19 April 2000, the acquisition would strengthen BAE Systems 'as a major player in the global defence market.'

BAE Systems' growing US presence played a part in the UK company's long-term strategy to become the world's leading defence manufacturer.

The British company's move into the US market was founded on the previous year's acquisition of Marconi, which meant the new company sold more to the DoD than the MoD. The takeover of Marconi Electronic Systems (MES) propelled BAE System into second place as a global defence contractor just behind Lockheed Martin and ahead of US groups Boeing and Raytheon. John Weston also pointed out that the acquisition of AES would establish his company as the number one in the world of electronic warfare systems and it would gain important supply positions in several key US defence programmes. These included the next generation of combat aircraft, the F-22 Raptor and the proposed Joint Strike Fighter (JSF), the Commanche helicopter, Virginia-class submarines and DD-21 destroyers. As John Weston put it, his group was now 'the leading American company in Europe and the leading European company in the United States.' (Forum Europe conference)

For Lockheed Martin, which had issued a series of profit warnings and seen a collapse in its share price over the previous 15 months, Chairman Vance Coffman admitted the AES transaction 'advances our strategic initiatives to refocus the corporation, generate cash and reduce debt.' Lockheed Martin had a defence turnover in 1998 of $16.6 billion, ahead of a combined BAE/Marconi turnover of $16.4 billion, with Boeing in third place at $15.6 billion. The AES takeover will consolidate BAE Systems' position as one of the strongest second tier systems and component suppliers in the United States, the world's largest defence market (Edgecliffe and Parkes 2000).

Certainly, as far as the new BAE Systems was concerned, continental companies were wary of being submerged in a British-dominated enterprise. The new BAE Systems, post Marconi (but not including AES), had defence sales of $16 billion, while DASA, Aerospatiale, Finmeccanica of Italy, Saab of Sweden and CASA of Spain had total revenues of $8.54 billion, $9.38 billion, $8.68 billion, $1.09 billion and $0.79 billion respectively in 1997. Some find it hard to imagine that the British government would fail to award a major defence contract to its national champions, which according to some Americans, would absorb half the UK's procurement budget. In May 1999, John Weston, BAE Systems' Chief Executive, estimated that BAE Systems would take around 25-30 per cent of the UK's procurement budget.

Weston confirmed that the new BAE Systems would sell more in the US than the UK, and already employed 21,000 people in continental Europe, 18,500 in the US, 5,500 in Saudi Arabia, 3,500 in Australia in addition to 70,000 in the UK.

Despite the initial reaction to the BAE Systems/Marconi deal, cross-border European defence integration soon picked up. In fact, BAE Systems' bold move galvanised continental defence companies into a competitive response. This has included the merger of DASA with CASA (Construcciones Aeronauticas), the joint venture between Westland and Augusta, the acquisition of Racal by Thomson-CSF, and the creation of the new European Aeronautic, Defence and Space Company (EADS), announced by DASA and Aerospatiale-Matra in October 1999. The presence of Chancellor Schroder and Prime Minister Jospin at the launch indicated the political symbolism attached to the Franco-German initiative. Siegmar Mosdorf, minister in the German Economics Ministry, said a combined European defence company was needed as:

> There is a political dimension to it...if we want to take responsibility for ourselves on foreign and security policy questions without being dependent on permanent help from the other side of the Atlantic.

A senior German official took a similar position: 'The ESDI cannot fly unless we give it wings. Those wings need to be provided by industry. Tony Blair seems very serious, but it needs something from the industry side' (Nicoll and Atkins 1999). EADS, which formally came into being on 10 July 2000, was the Franco-German response, without the participation of the British. However, EADS remained only the fifth largest defence contractor, well behind the top four (Lockheed Martin, BAE, Boeing and Raytheon).

EADS's flotation in July 2000 was less than a resounding success, with the company forced to slash its flotation price from an expected 24 euros to a closing price of just 17.50, valuing EADS at $13.5 billion. Complex shareholder and management structures, the cost of developing the A3XX jumbo jet, combined with the threat of fierce competition from the US, put off institutional investors.

A positive development arising from the EADS share floatation was the parallel agreement of the four Airbus Industrie partners to combine their operations into a single integrated company on 23 June 2000, an idea first mooted 13 years previously. The proposal repeatedly ran into political and corporate opposition, particularly in Germany and France, where governments and companies sought to keep control of their national aerospace and defence industries. The merger of the three other Airbus partners (DASA, CASA and Aerospatiale) to form the EADS was an undoubted stimulus to end the deadlock. The new Airbus Integrated Company (AIC), responsible for building and selling the hugely successful civil Airbus, transformed the old consortium structure under which the partners had kept their engineering and production assets separate. BAE Systems owned 20 per cent of the new company (AIC), with EADS left with a controlling 80 per cent. With Noel Forgeard installed as Chief Executive, BAE systems secured a veto over strategic decisions, and a right to sell its holding after three years. The latter was described as a 'nuclear hand-grenade' by John Weston, designed to act as a 'protection against deadlock in the joint venture.' AIC itself was to be governed by French law and headquartered in Toulouse. Overall, BAE Systems shared 67 per cent of EADS's total revenue (through Airbus, Eurofighter, Astrium and MBD), while only 25 per cent of BAE's revenue was shared with EADS, indicating the UK group's increased global presence, with nearly 70 per cent of its revenue coming from outside Europe and Britain.

However, in a bitter disappointment for BAE Systems and the British government, which had sought an Anglo-Italian industrial alliance, Finmeccanica announced it was joining forces with EADS to produce military and civilian aircraft. BAE Systems had been wooing the Italian company in order to create a pan-European alliance between the UK, Italy and Sweden to match the EADS grouping. The Finmeccanica-EADS deal envisaged a 50-50 tie-up on military aircraft, with the formation of a joint venture called the European Military Aircraft Company (EMAC). The new company was to have a 63 per cent stake in the Eurofighter project, leaving BAE Systems with a 37 per cent share. EADS won over Finmeccanica with a promise of a five per cent share in Airbus, with a guarantee that participation would provide jobs for Italy's aerostructures factory near Naples, in the country's impoverished South.

The BAE/Marconi and EADS mergers created two major European system integrating defence companies, with the assets and know-how to integrate advanced defence technology into European defence capabilities. The two merged companies were linked by a complicated web of cross-border relationships. BAE Systems owned German Plessy Systems, 50 per cent of Matra BAe Dynamics (MBD) and 49 per cent of German STN Atlas Electronik. GEC/Marconi owned 49.9 per cent of Matra Marconi Space, 49.9 of Thomson Marconi Sonar, and 50 per cent of Alenia Marconi Systems. French company Lagardere owned 50 per cent of MBD and 31 per cent of Matra Marconi Space (Adams, 1999).

The trend towards joint programmes and joint ventures ties BAE Systems and EADS together, and these relationships are now being rationalised. MBD and Thomson-CSF were the leading missile firms before the mergers, but operated in a crowded field. In October 1999, Aerospatiale/Matra, British Aerospace and Alenia Marconi Systems (a missile subsidiary of Finmeccanica and joint venture with Marconi), all agreed to combine these activities into Matra BAe Dynamics (MBD), leaving just two major integrators of missile systems. MBD became a transnational missile company, bigger than Lockheed Martin and second only to US giant Raytheon. Rationalisation in Europe's missile sector will dramatically improve European competitiveness in the global defence market. Thomson-CSF's response to the creation of MBD was to seek a 'common understanding' with Raytheon on plans for a joint venture in ground-based air defence systems. This would have the added advantage of hopefully opening up the US market to the French company (Nicoll, 2000b).

European companies are coalescing around two groupings in both satellites and helicopters. In helicopters, EADS's Eurocopter will be pitted against the Anglo-Italian Augusta-GKN Westland, while in satellites, Aerospatiale Matra, DASA and Marconi (BAE Systems), have created a joint subsidiary combining their space businesses (satellite communications, earth observation, space science, launchers such as Ariane and orbital infrastructure) into Astrium. The other satellite grouping is based around Alcatel-Thomson Space. BAE Systems is also merging its defence systems business (land and naval raiders, C2, simulation and air traffic control) with the work of Alenia Marconi Systems.

On the helicopter front, the AugustaWestland merger grew out of the agreement in March 1999 between GKN Westland of the UK and Finmeccanica, the state-controlled Italian company, to merge their two helicopter manufacturers. At the time, the merger was welcomed by then Defence Secretary George Robertson , who said: 'There is an urgent need to restructure Europe's aerospace industry to ensure that it can compete effectively in global markets and contribute to the strengthening of European defence.' Following the accord signed at the Farnborough Air Show on 26 July 2000, the two companies finally agreed the terms for the merger, which required approval from the EU's competition authorities. AugustaWestland, the 50:50 venture, had combined 1999 revenues of more than $2.1 billion (£1.4 billion) and an order book of $8 billion. According to estimates, AugustaWestland would have been the world's second largest helicopter manufacturer in 1999, (with 20 per cent of the world market) having sales of $1.35 billion, behind Boeing's £1.5 billion, but ahead of Eurocopter (£1.2 bn), Bell (£950 m) and Sikorsky (£875m). Eurocopter is a subsidiary of EADS, and Sikorsky is part of United Technologies. However, industry executives expect that the world's helicopter sector, itself a niche market in the aerospace industry, will experience further consolidation as demand is insufficient to support five major manufacturers.

European industrial consolidation and privatisation has been less marked in shipbuilding and land combat systems (such as tanks and armoured personnel carriers). Shipyards have consolidated at the national level in France and the UK, but are seen as insufficiently profitable, and supported by state subsidies on the continent. Fears that a £300 million MoD contract for six roll-on, roll-off ferries could be lost to European or Far East rivals caused consternation in the British shipbuilding industry in June 2000. BAE Systems, which acquired yards at Barrow-in-Furness, Cumbria, Scotstoun and Govan, both on the Clyde, suggested the future of Govan depended on winning the MoD order. Mersey-based Cammell Laird and Belfast's Harland and

Woolf held talks about a joint contract to build the transport ships, while Swan Hunter on Tyneside also hoped to gain work from the winning consortium. The British MoD subsequently asked the shipping consortia to re-submit their bids, but there were still concerns that European yards (especially Germany) were offering lower prices. For its part, the MoD said it was constrained by European Union public procurement rules, and the need to obtain value for money. The winning bidder would own and operate the ships, providing a service to the MoD under private finance initiatives.

British shipbuilding was undoubtedly helped by the decision of the MoD to place a £1 billion order for three of its 12 new Type 45 destroyers (all Royal Navy warships are built in Britain), with BAE Systems and Vosper Thorneycroft. The first two destroyers were planned to be built at BAE's Scotstoun yard, and by Vosper at either Southampton and Portsmouth. Sections of the ships would be built at different locations (spreading the work around) before being built on Clydeside or the south coast. Govan's longer-term prospects were helped by the MoD's plan to build the Type 45 destroyers in modular steel sections, particularly since BAE Systems was chosen as the prime contractor. The MoD announced the Type 45 programme would sustain up to 5,500 jobs in BAE Systems Marine and Vosper Thorneycroft shipyards, and in other defence industries in the UK.

Coming into service in 2007, the new Type 45 destroyers will be equipped with the Principal anti-air missile system (Paams) developed jointly by Britain, France and Italy, and designed to counter modern anti-ship missiles. The MoD described the new ships as a 'general purpose platform capable of operations across the spectrum of tasks from peace support to high intensity warfare.' The Paams system could give air support to British forces engaged in land battle, while the destroyers could also carry 200 marines and be equipped with Tomahawk cruise missiles. Yet the agonising over the MoD Ro-Ro order underlined the desperate state of the British shipbuilding industry, exemplified by Harland and Woolf's parlous financial state and order book and its decision to axe half its 1,250 workers in September 2000. There were calls from both within industry and from the trade union movement for the Government to devise a strategy for the British shipbuilding industry, before its remaining yards went to the wall. As Sir Richard Evans, BAE chairman said: 'We're interested in determining with the government what it is they want in the long term in capacity terms. We need to know what the future is for this business.' As a matter of urgency, the Government, working with the industry, trade unions, MoD and DTI should establish a framework document providing a strategic focus for rationalisng and consolidating the shipbuilding industry over the next 15 years (Nicoll, 2000c).

Land system firms in Europe have consolidated very slowly, with UK firm Alvis taking the lead. After Vickers' closure of the former Royal Ordnance factory at Leeds last year, there are only two tanks factories left in Britain. The two sole factories are

68   European defence

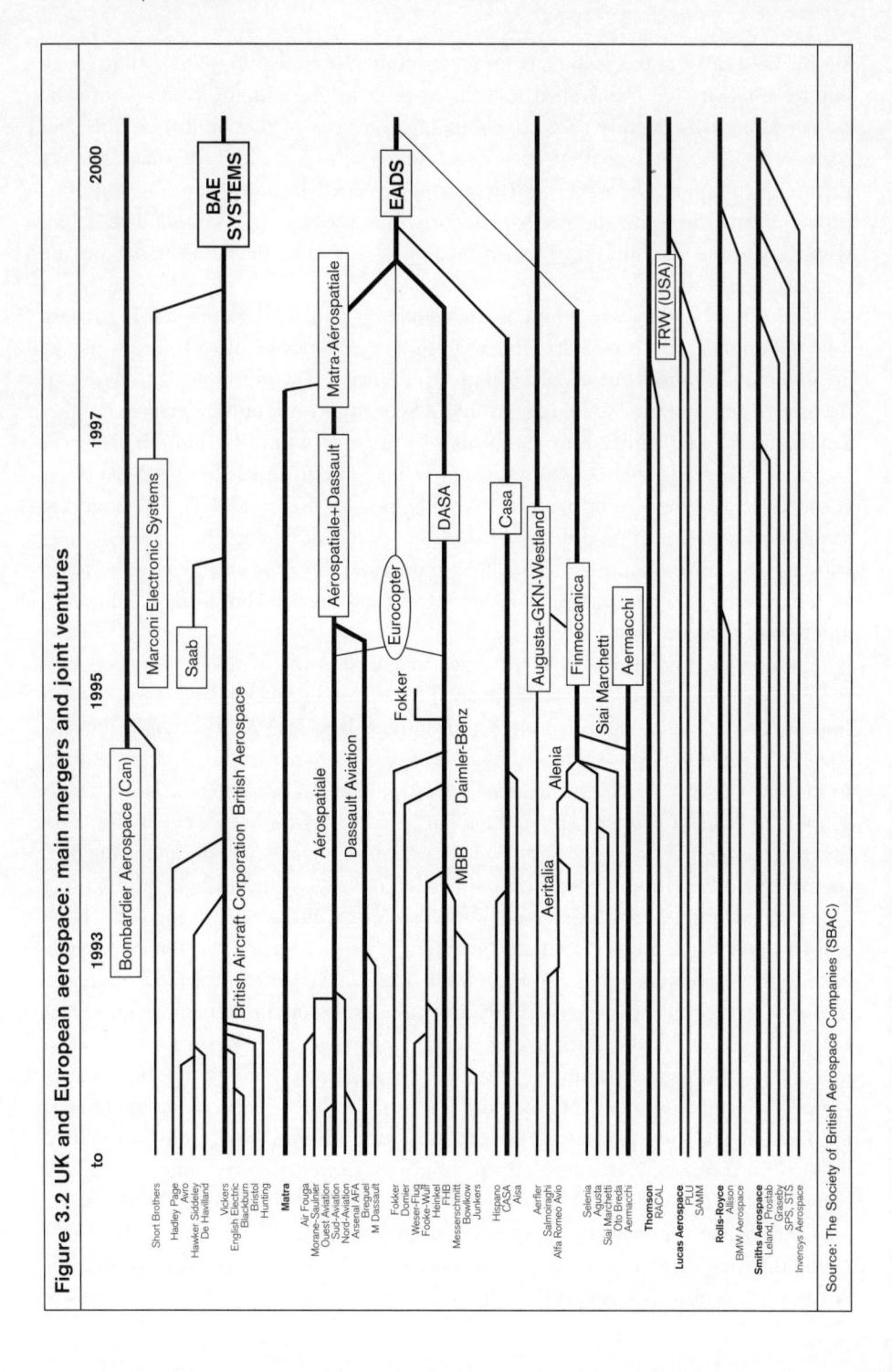

Figure 3.2 UK and European aerospace: main mergers and joint ventures

Source: The Society of British Aerospace Companies (SBAC)

Vickers' mile-long battle tank factory at Newcastle (now owned by Rolls-Royce after the RR-Vickers deal), and the former GKN plant at Telford in Shropshire, now owned by Alvis, which closed its Coventry factory in 1999. The lack of export orders for Vickers' Challenger 2 tank, supplied to the British Army, is disappointing for the company. As elsewhere in the defence sector, European over-capacity does not help, with three major battle-tanks (Challenger, Germany's Leopard and the French Leclerc), three German tank firms, and Giat in France producing tanks at an inefficient rate. Giat has formed a strategic partnership with Vickers on marketing, design and development, but the problem of over-capacity remains. Meanwhile Vickers has also announced a string of foreign partnerships, including with Singapore Technologies. A solution would be for the European tank manufacturers to consider a joint venture to produce the next generation of main battle tank (MBT), when in 20-30 years the existing generation are obsolete and need replacing. It would be helpful if the EU Member States could agree joint procurement requirements for the next generation battle tank, with France, Germany and Britain at the core of the joint programme, perhaps through OCCAR or a European Armaments Agency, if one ever comes into being. Failure to consolidate the tank sector will almost certainly lead to oblivion for that part of the defence industry, in the face of more effective and efficient US competition. Moves are likely in the UK at some stage to combine the operations of the two tank manufacturers. Below the MBT level, the picture for lighter armoured vehicles is not so bleak, with the British Army for example needing a succession of new vehicles to replace ageing stock.

Fortress Europe vs Fortress America

The current debate in political and defence circles about avoiding a 'Fortress Europe vs Fortress America' is an important one. For Europe, it is vital to maintain and develop access to the vast US market, and to gain the benefits of technology transfer. The EU defence initiative and European defence consolidation has been a political and economic response to the US overwhelming military and industrial dominance. Major procurement decisions in Europe (Eurofighter, Meteor and the military airbus A400M) are increasingly taken with regard not just for traditional national interests, but the interests of maintaining the EU's industrial defence base. The EU's leaders have been heavily influenced by the need to ensure that the CESDP is supported by a globally competitive European defence sector. The US has become alarmed that Europe may not just become politically decoupled from America, but industrially too. Buying American major defence equipment is becoming increasingly politicised. At the same time, the Europeans realise that simply buying-off-the-shelf from the US in all instances will bury the dream of an autonomous CESDP. Yet for both sides, the consequences of separation into separate fortresses is dire. For Europe, it would close off a major market, and circumscribe technological transfer. For the US, it could ultimately lead o the decoupling of the Atlantic Alliance, loss of market share, and damage investment prospects. Both Europe and the US would lose the benefit of growing transatlantic industrial partnerships between their respective defence companies.

The moves towards European defence integration have not been ignored by the United States. Fearful of the creation of a 'Fortress Europe' in the defence market, America has been keen to maintain the option of transatlantic partnerships in the defence sphere. A litmus test of US resolve (and concern) was the American offer for Britain to collaborate on the development of its Amraam, the widely-used AIM-120 advanced medium-range air-to-air missile made by Raytheon. The catch was that the principal weapon of the Eurofighter would be US made, and would eliminate the rival Meteor missile being developed by a consortium led by Matra BAe Dynamic (MBD), a joint venture started by BAE Systems and Lagardere. Boeing subsequently joined the Meteor team of European companies competing against Raytheon. It was estimated that the British share of the Meteor, the programme favoured by Germany, France and Italy, would be about £1 billion. The Meteor missile was planned to come into service from 2008. President Bill Clinton ensured that the decision to arm the 232 Eurofighters with either a US or European missile would be highly political, when he wrote to Tony Blair in August 1999:

> I believe transatlantic defence industry co-operation is essential to ensuring the continued interoperability of Allied armed forces, the importance of which was underscored in the recent NATO air campaign against Serbia. (Maguire and Gow, 2000)

Later President Clinton wrote a second time to the British Prime Minister, putting the case for Raytheon's Amraam, and underlining the phrase 'I feel strongly' about the decision in his letter (Morgan, 2000).

But Tony Blair had also been heavily lobbied by French President Jacques Chirac, German Chancellor Gerhard Schroder, Prime Minister Lionel Jospin and Prime Minister Jose-Maria Aznar of Spain. President Chirac started his letter 'Cher Tony' (Morgan, 2000), and remarked that it would be a 'shame if they [EU countries] were to make different choices, especially when the European product has the necessary performance and capability' Chirac made the case that the Meteor programme provided an opportunity for Europe to develop a common defence capability, in contrast to past failures at cooperation. He also indicated the British decision on the Beyond Visual Range Air-to-Air Missile (BVRAAM) would be crucial to the weapon's future, and added:

> I know your commitment to European construction. I am convinced that with your decision you will personally want to allow us together to give a powerful and concrete sign towards the European creation of a European defence identity (Odell, 2000).

Tony Blair's political credibility in Europe, and his leadership on the issue of enhancing European defence capabilities, was on the line. Economically, with the UK providing up to 35 per cent of the development £450 million development costs, Meteor would not have been viable without British support. Five European leaders had made representations to Blair, objecting to the use of a US missile on the Eurofighter. The £900 million contract would create or sustain 1,200 British jobs (according to BAE), challenge US hegemony in the missile sector (the US had never bought European missiles) and produce a cutting-edge 'ramjet' missile, which could travel at 3,000 mph and three times the range of current missiles (100km). At the Paris Air Show in June 1999, the Russians company Vympel displayed a ramjet powered long-range version of its AA-12, showing that they were also developing the ramjet technology, which takes in air through side vents in the missile. Against that, the US argued the case for interoperability, and offered the UK an unprecedented opportunity to share US classified technology and (with a 50 per cent share in all future air-to-air missiles for the Eurofighter) and at half the price of Meteor (£450 million). Additionally, Raytheon promised to upgrade the Amraam. The sting in the tail here was that the Americans would be able to veto the export (outside Europe) of Eurofighter and its weapons systems. This was not popular with the four nations building Eurofighter (Germany, Italy, Spain and Britain), or the other Meteor partners like France and Sweden, who would see their efforts to build an independent weapons capability founder. The BVRAAM was also intended to be used on Eurofighter,

Sweden's Gripen and France's Rafale, which could mean that all three European fighters would be offered the same Raytheon missile. Raytheon countered that its AMRAAM missile was in service with 16 nations and approved for 22, including Saudi Arabia and most of NATO, so it would be 'inconceivable' that there would be a country where Eurofighter nations could not export an AMRAAM-equipped Eurofighter. In a letter to Clinton in February 2000, Blair was desperate to avoid portraying the impending decision as a 'Fortress Europe versus Fortress America' conflict. The Prime Minister wrote:

> I am determined that the decision should not be seen as a 'Europe versus US' choice. The fact that, as you point out, Raytheon are teamed with a number of European companies, and that Boeing are allied with the competing consortium should help in that regard. (Odell, 2000)

Boeing's participation in the Meteor bid was disparaged by US defence Secretary Bill Cohen, who wrote to his British counterpart Geoff Hoon that Boeing's role with Meteor hardly amounted to true transatlantic co-operation: 'There has been a misconception that because Boeing has lent their name to the Meteor team there is "US involvement"'. Boeing management in Seattle were said to be 'incandescent' with rage about the comments. The Boeing contribution would be with respect to systems and aircraft integration and lean manufacturing techniques, rather than manufacturing itself. The Boeing-Meteor partnership was also linked to Boeing's desire to avoid giving Raytheon a monopoly position on a future missile contract for the proposed US Joint Strike Fighter (JSF).

Although discussed by the MoD's Equipment Approvals Committee, in effect the final decision on BVRAAM lay with the Prime Minister, who chairs the Cabinet's defence and overseas policy committee. At the end of the day, no-one outside the MoD believed the decision could be anything but highly political. The final outcome in favour of Meteor in May 2000 appeared almost inevitable in terms of reinforcing Britain's position at the heart of the push to enhance European defence capabilities, strengthening Europe's defence industries (especially its missile sector), maximising jobs in Europe, and giving the Europeans an opportunity to develop an autonomous high-tech weapons capability. Nevertheless, the terms agreed by the MoD on Meteor were extremely stringent, with Defence Secretary Geoff Hoon warning that if the programme did not develop as hoped 'the contract will be terminated by the partner nations who will recover all development costs from the contractor.' As ever with such a large programme, the MoD was trying to cover itself against massive cost overruns and severe delays, which have occurred in some major programmes in the past.

Raytheon, however, did not come away from the competition completely empty-handed. The MoD made a £200 million order for proven Raytheon missiles, to cover the period before the planned introduction of Meteor.

The BVRAAM contract also coincided with another crucial decision of whether to go down the path of a European programme or simply buy 'off-the-shelf', probably American, equipment. The issue was military transport aircraft, providing the strategic lift the Europeans so lacked in Kosovo. The RAF had already suffered a two-year delay by Lockheed Martin in supplying 25 C-130Js to replace the first half of the old Hercules fleet. In a choice between the military airbus A400M, Boeing's C-17, the C-130J Hercules and the Ukrainian Antonov 124, the MoD came up with what they felt was a practical solution, and others saw as a classic fudge. The MoD agreed to lease four C-17 heavy lift aircraft to transport armoured cars, helicopters and other equipment to crisis regions where British troops intervened, and for the longer-term ordered 25 A400Ms from Airbus. The decision to lease the C-17s for seven years gave the Boeing aircraft its first export customer. The A400M, although smaller than the C17, can carry heavier loads (but not a main battle tank). Sir Robert Walmsley, chief of defence procurement, said the cheaper Antonov was rejected because of 'operational issues' and questions about its reliability. However, the MoD had been chartering Antonov 124s for 10 years, although Russia had opposed their use in *Operation Allied Force*. Undoubtedly political and strategic factors played a part in rejecting the Ukrainian-made alternative, which was about £300 million less than budgeted for by the MoD. The military airbus order was subject to sufficient orders for the military airbus coming from other European states (failing that, the MoD would buy C-17s). The latter condition was soon met, with Germany, France, Italy, Spain, Turkey and Belgium, lifting the total commitment above the 180 threshold. The two MoD orders for Meteor and the A400M were worth £5 billion and created or safeguarded (according to BAE) around 5,000 British jobs, with the A400M alone creating about 3,000 new jobs.

The argument about transatlantic versus European industry is by no means clear-cut. European companies have been concerned to gain access to the US market, especially UK companies like BAE Systems, Rolls-Royce and the former GEC-Marconi. Rolls-Royce and GEC Marconi became considerable players in the American defence sector by acquiring engine maker Allison and defence electronics company Tractor respectively. Rolls-Royce is an example of a company with extensive civil and military transatlantic businesses and partnerships, embracing Lockheed Martin (C-130J Hercules), Airbus A330, Boeing (civil and military engines) and the Joint Strike Fighter (JSF) (Rolls Royce 2000).

BAE Systems, now incorporating Marconi, has both a relationship with Lockheed Martin on the JSF and Tracer armoured scout vehicle (under threat of being axed), and with Boeing on its rival JSF bid. Thomson-CSF is developing a joint venture with Raytheon in air defence systems. EADS was actively courting the US's Northrop Grumman, Lockheed Martin has discussed developing links with Aerospatiale and Airbus, while Boeing and BAE Systems were denying that a merger was imminent. UK defence firm Lucas also merged into the US market and is now part of TRW. Overall, continental European firms were less successful that British companies in acquiring or establishing partnerships in the American market. Aerospatiale sold off its holding of Fairchild in the early 1990s, and Thomson-CSF bid to acquire Vought Aerospace was unsuccessful in 1993 (as was EADS's attempt to purchase Lockheed's Sanders).

Similarly, US prime contractors were seeking European partners to access the European market. Three US prime contractors bid for the UK's £750 million Airborne Stand-off Radar (ASTOR) programme, with Lockheed Martin, Raytheon Systems Limited and Northrop Grumman competing fiercely to attract British companies as partners. There should be no illusion that this was for political, rather then technical reasons, as the primes (especially the winner Raytheon), were perfectly capable of producing ASTOR without UK expertise.

With the exception of Raytheon's presence in the UK, where it employs over 2,500 people at nearly a dozen sites, there are few significant European defence assets which have been purchased by US firms. However, the US General Electric company participates in a joint venture with French firm SNECMA, marketing the CFM-56 engine. Boeing has also purchased the Czech aircraft company Aero Vodochody, in anticipation of winning orders from the new Central and East European members of NATO.

The New Labour Government was careful not to demand European defence integration at the cost of transatlantic partnerships. The former Defence Secretary, George Robertson, told the *Defence Review* in the autumn of 1998 that although he felt the only way forward for the UK defence industry lay in consolidation with their European rivals:

> We're going rapidly in a direction where there simply will be no choice. There will be two American manufacturers who will produce two different sets of products and nobody will have any choice, even the Americans.
>
> The situation where we have big, national companies, essentially depending on national markets can't go on. In a decade, people won't be buying expensive aeroplanes when they can choose competitive – ruthlessly competitive – American products.
>
> But we're not arguing here for a Fortress Europe, some new Atlantic wall between the States and Europe in terms of who buys what where. Big British companies which are highly competitive, highly successful, have got connections across the Atlantic. So there is a bridge in both directions (Robertson, 1998).

No major British defence or aerospace company wishes to see a Fortress Europe develop, neither would they welcome a Fortress America. Yet many obstacles to a free flow of transatlantic trade, technology, partnerships and acquisition remain. On the

US side, the obstacles include the 'Buy America Act' and regulations that favour US suppliers, reluctance to share technology, restrictions on foreign firms that acquire US defence companies, complicated and bureaucratic export regulations, the influence of Congress and the power of the military-industrial complex.

In most cases, foreign investment in the US defence industry must be approved by the Committee on Foreign Investment in the United States (CFIUS), comprising 11 agencies including the DoD, Department of Commerce and the Treasury. Under the Exon-Florio Amendment to the Defense Production Act of 1950, the US Government reviews and can block the acquisition and control of an American company by a foreign national (or company) for national security reasons. The Hart-Scott-Rodino Antitrust Improvements Act of 1976 requires parties intending to merge or acquire another entity to give advance notice to the Federal Trade Commission and the Antitrust Division of the Department of Justice, if the transaction meets certain thresholds. All the forgoing makes doing business in America difficult, getting export licences problematic and selling into the market sometimes impossible. There is a real fear that that the US is capable of vetoing exports from a US-European joint venture which conflicted with American strategic interests or the interests of a major US prime. The close relationship between Congress and the US military-industrial complex and the 'pork barrel' factor exacerbate these concerns.

On the European side, the US complains of state subsidies, protected markets, and lack of cohesion in export regulations, procurement requirements and industrial policy. However, even 'protectionist' France has bought US early-warning aircraft, and the EU imports 50 per cent of its defence equipment from overseas, while the US imports only three per cent of its defence requirements (mainly from the UK). Some 80 per cent of European defence imports are from the US, America's most important market outside the Middle East, with EU-American defence trade in the US's favour by a margin of 7:1. The US is therefore the main (but not sole) beneficiary in the transatlantic defence trade.

From its side of the Atlantic, Washington has at least started to address some of these issues.

One of the most serious impediments for any European company acquiring a US defence firm is the DoD's requirement for a 'proxy board' of US nationals to run the enterprise in a way that safeguards US security. This causes problems for European companies, who fear that in effect they will not run their own US-based enterprise. It is also not matched by any similar requirement for US companies who buy into the European market. However, in January 2000, the DoD signalled a relaxation of this requirement in the case of Allison, the engine maker purchased by Rolls-Royce. Instead of a 'proxy board', a 'Special Security Agreement' would cover the company, so that Allison would only require one US official with security clearance sitting on the board, with several others acting as non-executive directors. The US government further eased some of the restrictions for Rolls-Royce on personnel visitation and technology transfer. BAE Systems North America is also required to operate at arms length from its parent group, and is governed by a separate group intended to assure the US government US technology secrets will be protected. The board of the American offshoot of BAE includes retired senior US servicemen, as well as John Weston and Mike Turner, BAE chief operating officer. However, the two Britons are not members of a government security sub-committee of the board, which can only include US citizens. Nonetheless, Jacques Gansler, the Pentagon's procurement chief says of BAE Systems: 'We treat them as a US defence company.' This attitude reflects the fact that BAE operates in 26 out of the 50 states in the America, is already recognised as an important second tier US group, and employs 18,300 people there. Gansler confirmed the terms of some US security agreements would be relaxed, and he recognised that 'most firms are globalised and the technology is globalised, so we should take advantage of that and not fight it.' Yet restrictions on technology transfer have been tight, with British firms working on the US Joint Strike Fighter (JSF) compelled to build 'firewalls' in their UK plants to prevent technology leakage, and British companies barred from several key JSF project meetings.

Security agreements themselves are common in Europe as well as in the US, and recent examples have included the acquisition of Racal Electronics by Thomson-CSF. In the latter case, Thomson-CSF and the MoD signed an agreement in which Thomson undertook to protect classified information and to consult the MoD on any changes to Racal's defence activities affecting the UK's national security interests. GKN AugustaWestland is also subject to a less formal security agreement. It is clear that the Allison arrangements reflect the close working relationship and trust built up between Roll-Royce, the DoD and the US defence sector over a number of years, and the special arrangements offered to Rolls-Royce will only be extended to other non-US companies on a case-by-case basis. The DoD initiative nevertheless indicates a new degree of flexibility from the DoD, and is a vote of confidence and trust in UK firms who have made acquisitions in the United States. Yet while the DoD welcomes further transatlantic investment, partnership, joint ventures or projects and smaller acquisitions, it still draws the line at a major merger between a European prime and a US counterpart. Nor can a European defence company act as a prime contractor in the US market.

The Pentagon has made it quite clear that following the move to block Lockheed Martin's acquisition of Northrop Grumman, it will not allow a major transatlantic merger or takeover (say between Boeing and BAE Systems). This is both for reasons of national strategic interest, and to retain competition in the US defence market. According to Sir Richard Evans, BAE Systems chairman, a merger between BAE and Boeing or Lockheed Martin was 'completely impossible' for the foreseeable future. BAE has a very strong relationship with Boeing, which has built the UK Harrier and

Hawk aircraft under licence, and was involved in BAE's Nimrod patrol aircraft and Meteor missile programmes. Sir Richard said big US mergers were 'inconceivable' because the DoD and State Department were not ready for them. Top Pentagon officials were also worried about the health of some US defence companies. In the case of Lockheed Martin, another disincentive complicating any merger would be the US company's $12 billion (£7.8 bn) debt load. In fact, the profitability of some of the US defence giants was so bad after consolidation that Lockheed Martin warned they would not survive unless the Pentagon paid them more for their products. Vince Coffman, Lockheed's chairman, insisted the company's problems over the past year or so (including a series of profit warnings and collapsed share price) reflected a deeper malaise. Vince Coffman told the *Financial Times*:

> When you see that three of the four major prime contractors in the US have bond ratings that are BBB-, you know there's a problem in the industry. This is not a one-company phenomenon (Nicoll, 2000d).

Lockheed Martin, like its rivals Boeing and Raytheon, grew substantially during the 1990s wave of acquisitions encouraged by the Pentagon, but all ran into financial difficulties (although Boeing has now turned the corner). Lockheed suffered particular problems with rocket launchers and the C-130J Hercules. Coffman complained most of the savings created by the mergers had been absorbed by the US Government, without benefiting the companies. To rectify the situation, he called on the US authorities to improve contractors' cash position by increasing the 'progress payments' made by the Pentagon during the life of a contract. Under the Pentagon's cost-plus contracting system (abandoned by the UK as inefficient and a licence for contractors to print money), companies submit invoices for costs incurred at various stages of a programme, and the government reimburses 75 per cent of the costs in progress payments. Not satisfied with this cosy arrangement, Coffman argued that this level should be increased to 85 or 90 per cent. The profitability position of several of the US primes showed there was a down-side to consolidation, and contrary to widespread belief, bigger did not necessarily mean more efficient, profitable or better. Yet it is hard to imagine that the drive to dominate a shrinking global defence market with over-capacity will altogether cease. Below the top US prime contractors, for example, there is still considerable scope for further industrial consolidation. The fundamental laws of supply and demand, to achieve cost savings and penetrate overseas markets will also inevitably reduce the number of companies able to compete on a global scale. In time, further transnational and transatlantic mergers are likely, although this will require changes in attitudes and policies on both sides of the Atlantic. As John Weston, BAE CEO told *Defence Review* in the summer of 1999:

We're looking at a process the end of which will be the globalisation of the industry. It will have two or three major players that will lead the industry internationally in the way that two of three lead in the US today (Hawkey and Winfield 1999).

Profitability, however, will remain an issue, and as the primes struggle to digest their latest acquisitions, they will have to grapple with achieving synergies in their businesses, divesting themselves of unprofitable or unrelated units, and ensuring they create satisfactory returns for their shareholders while managing the development risks associated with technological change. The danger is that globalisation of the defence sector could result in implosion if the defence primes over-extend themselves, sacrificing efficiency and profitability in the process.

More recently, there have been signs of a revival in the US aerospace industry, much to the relief of the US defence primes, with both Lockheed Martin and Northrop Grumman showing improved profitability in the second quarter of 2000.

Beginning in 1998, the US Deputy Secretary John Hamre initiated three separate investigations (the Defence Science Board, the Defence Policy Board and the Strategic Studies Group), into the policy implications of globalisation on the US defence sector and America's security interests. Of these three studies, the high-level Defence Science Board (DSB) report has been influential in shifting US policy towards a more flexible export regime and co-operation in technology transfer. The DSB report recognised that the US was increasingly unable to control the flow of technology across national borders, and the whole range of 'spin-in' technologies from the civilian sector (such as software and global communications) to the defence sector transcended the old ideas of a national defence industrial base. The DSB Task Force on Globalization and Security summed up these developments when its report was published in December 1999:

> Accordingly, US military-technological advantage will derive less from advanced component and subsystem technology developed by the US defense sector than from the military functionality generated by superior, though not necessarily US-based, defense sector systems integration skills.
> (DSB 1999)

The net result would be a dramatic increase in the DoD's use of commercial-off-the-shelf (COTS) components, subsystems and services, which may or may not originate in the US.

The effect of such globalisation would also enable the US's potential opponents to put together a range of capabilities, which although inferior to the US, would represent an 'asymmetric challenge.' The DSB Task Force made no effort to disguise

US strategy (and reality), with the findings and recommendations section of the report entitled 'Maintaining US Military Dominance Amidst Global Technological Levelling.' The report concluded that although the 'list of U.S controllable technologies is shrinking', the United States should endeavour to protect and preserve essential American technology (such as nuclear and some systems integration technologies, stealth and sensors), and ensure these must be produced in the 'US only.' In other words the US must prevent the most sensitive technologies from leaking abroad, and ensure they were only produced in the USA. The issue here was to more clearly define the essential military capabilities which the US felt it could not risk ending up in potentially hostile hands; with a foreign-owned, controlled or influenced (FOCI) firm; or even with its allies.

The DSB Task Force report was followed by the Anglo-US Declaration of Principles (DoP) signed in February 2000, which sought to improve co-operation on a range of subjects including market access, security of supply, exports, handling of classified information, R&T and military requirements. However, there was a policy dispute between the DoD and State Department (which is responsible for licensing exports of defence articles and services), with the latter reluctant to relinquish its tight control over defence exports. The policy confusion between the DoD and State Department caused some concern in British Government circles, and was only resolved when the White House intervened to knock heads together in the two departments, at the highest level. The US State Department's response was Madeleine Albright's announcement of the Defence Trade Security Initiative (DTSI) at the North Atlantic Council Ministerial in Florence on 24 May 2000. The US Secretary of State said:

> I am announcing today an important initiative by my government to improve transatlantic cooperation in the area of defense trade. The initiative is a package of seventeen specific steps aimed at getting US defense exports to NATO countries, Japan and Australia faster and more smoothly.

The DTSI went some way to deal with some of the problems experienced by European companies doing business with the United States. The US agreed to establish new ITAR (International Traffic in Arms Regulations) exemptions for unclassified defence items, data and services for qualified firms in allied countries with which it signed bilateral agreements, and had also adopted and demonstrated export controls and security systems comparable to the USA. The new ITAR licensing exemptions covered unclassified exports to foreign governments and companies who are identified as reliable by the US government, in consultation with foreign governments. The new approach would be applied to those US allies who provided reciprocity in exports and industrial security; long-standing and successful co-operation in intelligence- sharing and law enforcement; and guaranteed reciprocal market access. Among allied countries, the UK and Australia were singled out to launch the first set of negotiations, given their 'long history of co-operation in a number of relevant security areas, their compatible control and technology security systems and their significant industrial linkages with the US'.

The DTSI also included a range of flexible, new licensing vehicles, which will be established for NATO countries, Japan and Australia, that would allow 'one-stop' streamlined licensing (instead of the multiple licences now required), for government programmes and commercial sales to foreign governments, international co-operative programmes and commercial ventures. The DTSI 17-point plan envisaged the introduction of major programme and project licences, global project licences, enhancing the use of multiple destination licences, expedited licence review for NATO purchases, the extension of the ITAR exemption to qualified countries, exemption for DoD bid proposals and regular reviews of the US Munitions List. The major programme licence would provide a single comprehensive licence issued at the beginning of a project; a major project licence would provide a single comprehensive licence for a major sale of defence articles to NATO; and a global project would consist of a single licence to cover a government-to-government international agreement for a co-operative project.

Whilst welcomed by the defence industry, there is still a feeling that the DTSI only represents the beginning of a process to open up the US defence market and facilitate transfers of technology, rather than the end of the recurring problems experienced by European industry. Beyond the UK, there is also a question mark over when, and if, the US will extend any ITAR exemption to companies in the rest of Europe. There is, for example, still a degree of suspicion about the trustworthiness of France, which is not regarded as a reliable US ally when it comes to sharing secrets and sensitive technology. The US Congress is also reluctant to cede its powers in the field of approving exports of defence articles or services (valued over $14 million), and like the State Department, is engaged in a turf war with the DoD over this issue. While the State Department sees export licences and controls as a tool of US foreign policy and its global strategy, politicians in the US Congress sees their oversight role as a useful way of protecting the interests of the American military-industrial complex, and jobs in their homes states. The Congress versus Administration struggle over liberalising defence export licences and technology transfer, while not an issue of principle, is certainly a cause of conflict between a Democrat White House and a Republican-controlled Congress. Generally, however, the political and economic imperative is weighted in favour of liberalisation, as the US defence sector seeks to maintain and expand overseas markets, encourage investment and embrace transatlantic partnerships and joint ventures. Certainly, the US could not afford to ignore the reaction of European companies like DASA, which in October 1999 announced its staff should only buy European, rather than US components (especially goods for defence use), because of slow US government export control decisions. Even though over 99 per cent of all US export licenses are ultimately approved, the review time had stretched to the point that it was discouraging sales. The DSB Task Force reported:

- ITAR technology transfer and re-transfer regulations are often perceived by potential foreign investors as too restrictive, and the defense export licensing process too sluggish, for effective transnational operations.

- FOCI regulations and requirements are laborious for and disadvantageous to FOCI firms. (DSB, 1999)

The US desire to maintain American military supremacy was in danger of undermining that very supremacy, hence the change of heart in Washington.

Nevertheless, the US has to do more if it is serious about opening up the US defence market to further partnerships and joint ventures, liberalising the export regime and facilitating the transatlantic exchange of technology. First, the US needs to relax its proxy board requirements for foreign-owned US defence companies, and develop the more widespread use of 'special security agreements', similar to the one agreed in the case of engine-maker Allison (acquired by Rolls-Royce). The latter agreements would only be reached with countries and companies qualified for ITAR exemption, particularly regarding export controls, industrial security, intelligence sharing, law enforcement and market access.

There also needs to be a move to 'process-based' licensing. There should be a shift away from individual transactions towards certification of internal control procedures. Under this new approach to export controls, the US government would audit and certify the company's internal controls to comply with export restrictions. If certified as compliant, the company would be authorised to export without further transactional licensing. To ease bureaucracy, what is really required is a complete overhaul of the export licensing system, focusing on procedural implementation rather than export licence paper chasing, which is often lengthy and ineffective.

The current US National Disclosure Policy already includes an assessment of the sensitivity of the technology and the reliability of the trading partner. The disclosure policy could be improved, however. For example, in the case of a security agreement between two countries (along the lines of the Anglo-US Declaration of Principles), blanket exemptions could be applied to national disclosure policy. Another reform could be to establish a US government-industry consultation process. The current US export control process does not have an explicit and transparent procedure for industry consultation with government in advance of a licence submission, or for an appeal process.

The ITAR waiver agreed between the US and Canada, where unclassified components and data may be exchanged without licensing, should be applied to the UK and other eligible countries as soon as possible, particularly European NATO members. In addition, there should be a stronger partnership between US law enforcement agencies, customs, defence and intelligence agencies in the field of defence-related exports. Instead of relying on a licence to trigger an interagency review, the agencies should collaborate in advance to identify potentially suspect transactions and to notify companies to be on guard for specific purchase requests from suspect buyers. The US government has already started to establish such a system involving the Defense Department, the Justice Department, the FBI and Central Intelligence Agency, and this work should be expedited.

The proposed Presidential Commission on the future of the US aerospace industry should be extended to cover transatlantic defence relations, culminating in a European-US summit on the subject.

On the European side, EU efforts to define a single company law, industrial policy for the aerospace and defence sector and a common European export control regime should be redoubled, but should not discriminate against non-EU firms. OCCAR discussions on defining common defence procurement rules should also take the transatlantic dimension into account.

Conclusions and policy recommendations

- European tank manufacturers should consider a joint venture to produce the next generation of main battle tank (MBT), when in 20-30 years time the existing generation are obsolete and need replacing. EU Member States should agree joint procurement requirements for the next generation battle tank, with France, Germany and Britain at the core of a joint programme, managed either by OCCAR or the European Armaments Agency.

- As a matter of urgency, the Government, working with the industry, trade unions, MoD and DTI should establish a framework document providing a strategic focus for rationalising and consolidating the shipbuilding industry over the next 15 years (up to 2015).

- The US has to do more if it is serious about opening up the US defence market. The US needs to relax its proxy board requirements for FOCI firms, and develop the more widespread use of 'special security agreements', similar to the one agreed with Rolls-Royce over Allison.

- There needs to be a move to more 'process based' licensing in the US. There should be a shift away from individual transactions towards certification of internal control procedures, and a complete overhaul of the export licensing system, focusing on procedural implementation rather than licence 'paper chasing.'

- The current US National Disclosure Policy should be improved through, for example, blanket exemptions in the case of a security agreement between two countries. Another reform could be to establish a government-industry consultation and appeal process.

- The ITAR waiver agreed between the US and Canada, should be applied to the UK and other eligible countries as soon as possible, particularly European NATO members. In addition, there should be a stronger partnership between US law enforcement agencies, customs, defence and intelligence agencies in the field of defence-related exports.

- The proposed Presidential Commission on the future of the US aerospace industry should be extended to cover transatlantic defence relations, culminating in a European-US summit on the subject.

- EU efforts to define a single company law, industrial policy for the aerospace and defence sector and a common European export control regime should be redoubled, but should not discriminate against non-EU firms. OCCAR discussions on defining common defence procurement rules should also take the transatlantic dimension into account.

IV: Procurement issues

European armaments co-operation

The Amsterdam Treaty refers to the fact that the 'framing of a common defence policy will be supported, as Member States consider appropriate, by co-operation by them in the field of armaments' (Article J7). No single European country has a defence industry capable of meeting all its own requirements, and the capability to attempt to source most of a nation's own security needs is certain to decline. The move towards rationalisation and consolidation of the European defence industry is thus going to lead to increased joint sourcing and procurement of weapons systems. On the other hand, NATO and EU Member States have failed to agree on any common system of procurement, or as a first stage, agree on common force requirements. NATO has tried and failed to define common requirements for 50 years, witness the inability of NATO nations to agree on a single system of airborne ground surveillance. European co-operation in the armaments field has been of limited success, despite the formation of OCCAR, the WEAG and WEAO.

As previously noted, OCCAR was established in November 1996, involving Germany, France, Italy and the UK. A Convention formally establishing OCCAR as a body with a separate legal identity was signed by the four countries in September 1998, and laid before the UK's House of Commons for ratification in June 2000. The four OCCAR partners have reached agreement on the principles of acquisition for any management policy, including preference for equipment within the framework of OCCAR. They have agreed to do away with the concept of industrial reciprocity on a programme to programme basis (*juste retour*) and recognised the need for a full and comprehensive return over a long-term period. The abolition of juste retour, which automatically assures the industry of each country involved in a project a share of the work in direct relation to that country's financial contribution, is crucial. Juste retour is extremely uncompetitive and inefficient, and revolves around each country trying to get the best production deal for its industry, rather than prioritising the needs of the collaborative project. Almost all previous collaboration shave been based on *juste retour*, with variable outcomes. In contrast, the OCCAR Convention states:

> the Member States renounce, in their co-operation, the analytical calculation of industrial juste retour on a programme-by-programme basis, and replace it by the pursuit of an overall multi-programme/multi-year balance.

Currently OCCAR manages seven programmes (Hot, Milan, Roland, Brevel, Tiger, Cobra and FSAF), worth in excess of 17.5 billion euros. The integration of a further three programmes (AC3/MP, AC3G/LP and VCBI- GTK/MRAV without France), will bring the total up to €26.5 billion.

The Western European Armaments Group (WEAG) was formed in December 1992, and was designed to be a European armaments co-operation forum for all 13 European NATO members (the ten WEU nations plus Denmark, Norway and Turkey). In 1998, Austria, Finland and Sweden joined the group as observers. The WEAG develops European armaments co-operation through regular meetings of the National Armament Directors of the 13 member countries, who are answerable to their respective defence ministries. In the autumn of 1997, WEAG defence ministers directed their national armament directors to develop a plan to guide the way towards implementation of a European armaments agency. Previously, in autumn 1996, WEAG defence ministers approved the charter and signed the memorandum of understanding for the Western European Armaments Organisation (WEAO), with its executive body, the Research Cell. The WEAO was the first European armaments cooperation body with an international legal personality, which gives it the capacity to place contracts with the defence industry. Established in November 1996, the WEAO was designed to act as a precursor to the European Armaments Agency.

The European Armaments Agency (EAA) is still very much on the drawing-board. The idea for a European Armaments Agency was launched almost nine years ago. On 10 December 1991, in the Declaration of WEU member states on the role of the WEU and its relations with the EU and the Atlantic Alliance, ministers reached agreement on 'enhanced cooperation in the field of armaments with the aim of creating a European Armaments Agency.' The 'Masterplan for the European Armaments Agency' was developed in 1998, and at their meeting on 17 November, ministers agreed on the Masterplan as the basis of future developments and actions towards the EAA. Preparatory steps to establish the EAA are being taken forward by a group of national experts (GNE) from the WEAG nations , which would report to ministers in the autumn of 2001. The way OCCAR might work with the EAA was effectively being left until then.

The EAA's range of activities are planned to include research, procurement, studies, management of assets and other functions. The EAA's business strategy has to address the agency's commercial constitution and procedures (such as management techniques, philosophy and control) and acquisition strategies, which will have to be flexible to cope with the changing demands of each new project. The EAA's business strategy must also ensure the utmost efficiency in terms of an optimal cost-benefit ratio. The main tasks of the EAA would be to achieve the progressive harmonisation of equipment requirement and standardisation, and to rationalise the current ad hoc approach to European armaments co-operation. Establishing an EAA by 2003, by the time the European Rapid Reaction Force is fully operational, should be an EU priority. An effective EAA would enjoy many of the benefits of existing US procurement policy, such as a large research and development budget, long production runs and centralised project management. Such a policy would also bring economies of scale, vital to compete with the US defence sector and essential in reducing the unit-costs of equipment, and spiralling research and development costs. Real European armament co-operation, harmonisation and procurement, would increase efficiency, reduce costs, and underpin the European defence industrial base essential for an effective Common European Security and Defence Policy (CESDP).

However, the European field of armaments organisations is currently too crowded. The WEU's WEAG and WEAO should be wound-up over the next three years, and their responsibilities folded into NATO, as the WEU effectively ceases to exist. OCCAR should be retained for the time being and form the model for the operation of the EAA. EU Member States should only join the EAA when they are able to meet the obligations and responsibilities of OCCAR membership. The end result should be one European armaments agency representing EU Member States, with NATO seeking to achieve wider harmonisation and interoperability between EU and non-EU NATO members, Canada and the United States. In the meantime, OCCAR should be awarded management of further substantial programmes (in addition to the A400M military airbus), to enhance its credibility and status as Europe's leading collaborative armaments organisation, for example Meteor and a future EuroTank project.

The International Institute for Strategic Studies suggests that European equipment programmes frequently result in 'technical under-performance, delayed schedules, and substantial cost overruns.' While this is undoubtedly so, the IISS suggestion that the most promising solution lay in 'NATO-wide programmes, administered by central NATO procurement organisation and sourced from a competitive transatlantic defence industry' is frankly unworkable and politically unacceptable. Many Europeans are wary that such a proposal would merely be a front for the United States to sell its defence equipment to its European allies, under the guise of achieving standardisation and interoperability. The IISS itself recognises the problem, with the US-proposed NATO Conference of National Armament Directors (CNAD) remaining 'an ineffective forum for NATO armaments cooperation, since there is no consensus among NATO governments as to how the organisation should be further empowered.' The evolution of OCCAR and the development of the EAA are a more realistic and politically acceptable way forward for Europeans (IISS, 1999).

Smart procurement, competition and European harmonisation

The Labour Government has made a commitment to improve the overall level of weapons procurement. The main elements of this 'smart procurement' initiative are threefold: first, adopting new approaches to procurement, including a through-life systems approach; second, Introducing Integrated Project Teams (IPTs) to manage each project, with a greater focus on partnership with industry; third, simplifying procedures, and tailoring them to the different levels of complexity that projects can involve. The targets are a 30 per cent cost saving and a 50 per cent improvement in delivery times. Introducing commercial values into the process brings with it notions of partnership between buyer and customer and of creating long-term relationships between prime and subcontractors.

Geoff Hoon, UK Defence Secretary, pointed to several smart procurement successes in a speech to a Defence Exports Services Organisation (DESO) symposium on 22 March 2000 (see www.mod.uk/news/speeches). The Defence Secretary announced the Defence Procurement Agency (DPA) and GKN Westland had identified potential savings of £700 million over the projected 30-year life of the Apache aircraft. The Apache project was one of the first to form into an Integrated Project Team (IPT). The savings would come from capital investment in alternative support strategies over the life of the Apache helicopter, which had been delivered on time and on budget. In addition, Geoff Hoon stated that rationalisation of the UK's armoured fighting vehicle fleet would allow development of armoured capability at reduced time and cost, with the prospect of new vehicles being delivered to the front line four years earlier than previously envisaged. The plans had the potential to save up to £2 billion in the period 2010-20. Another success was the training system for the Hawk aircraft, which had been delivered to RAF Valley, on time and on budget (a budget 20 per cent lower than the conventional procurement route).

The MoD's Defence Logistics Organisation (DLO) came into operation on 2 April 2000, with General Sir Sam Cowan as its head. The DLO brings together the three single separate Service logistic support areas into a single tri-Service organisation employing 43,000 people. The primary aim of the new organisation was to cut costs, with the aim of reducing costs by 20 per cent within five years. Before the DLO, which was established as a result of the 1998 Strategic Defence review, the three Services had separate repair and supply organisations, working to separate sets of regulations, with three sets of information technology at different levels of development. The DLO's task was also to move away from a bureaucratic paper-chasing system to one based on e-commerce. These reforms would free-up resources for the front line, and help the DLO to play a key role in the implementation of smart procurement, opening up opportunities for closer co-operation between the MoD and industry.

Yet, despite the apparent successes of the smart procurement initiative, there have been some doubts expressed about how smart procurement works in practice. There have been some complaints from industry that the concept of 'partnership' stressed in the smart procurement initiative is rather one-sided, as the MoD seeks to shift the balance of development risk from government to the private sector. Another, more tangible concern is that the IPTs tend to look at the narrow picture, are too insular, and fail to examine the wider implications of any programme on industry. Nevertheless, Sir Robert Walmsley, UK Chief of Defence Procurement, believes that many of the principles of smart procurement could be incorporated into OCCAR's working practices, particularly the idea of IPTs. It is to be hoped that the IPTs themselves are more integrated into the MoD's consultative structures, so that they do not work in isolation on their projects, without regard to the broader picture of the industrial and economic impact of their work.

Bearing in mind that smart procurement is a relatively new initiative, the MoD should instigate a study of the effectiveness of the processes adopted, review progress so far, and consider any changes or improvements which might or might not be necessary. At the end of the day, the test for smart procurement will be to secure tangible and demonstrable improvements of project timescales and costs, over a measurable period.

However, the benefits of smart procurement may in any case be nugatory if it becomes impossible to deliver equally smart European procurement, as Professor Keith Hayward of the Society of British Aerospace Companies told a Forum Europe conference in Brussels on 23 April 1998:

> In the next decade, we are talking about a fully internationalised procurement process. The idea that the Brits alone can deliver smart procurements and savings is quite absurd... If changing attitudes at national level is difficult, changing attitudes at European level will be even more so.

The issue for the European defence industry is that before it can even consider participating in joint EU procurement, there must be political, military and strategic agreement on what is required when by Europe's armed forces. EU defence capability criteria can establish broad guidelines for levels of defence spending in GDP terms, and the proportion of defence budgets spent on R&D. What will be more difficult will be to agree on a strategic framework for the EU's new defence capabilities, and how they can meet the requirements of deployability and sustainability within the overall force structure. Exact equipment needs will have to be quantified on a multilateral basis, allowing for the principle of interoperability, both amongst the EU Member States and their non-EU NATO allies.

The MoD, like the DoD in the US, is determined to use competition in the defence industry to drive down the cost of procurement. In the UK, the government has gone further by abandoning the cosy 'cost plus' contracts, in which the supplier was paid the cost of the project plus a percentage profit. The changeover to a more commercial approach began with the appointment of Peter Levine, now Lord Levine of Portsoken, as Chief of Defence Procurement in the MoD in December 1984. Previously, contracts were placed by allocation rather than competition, with little incentive for suppliers to improve efficiency or innovate. Indeed, the greater the costs and delay, the higher the profit. Now, however, some voices are suggesting that competition has gone too far, with companies so desperate to win contracts that the firm which takes the greatest development risk and the lowest profit wins the bid. There is a danger that companies take more risk than is prudent, because the alternative of losing is so dire. The result can be poor performance, hitting profitability and earnings or even insolvency and job losses. Prime contractors are often asked to replace equipment on platforms late in the competitive process, also increasing risk. A competition like the Maritme Patrol Aircraft can take up to two years to decide, and cost the parties in excess of £100 million in bidding and assessment costs. In the case of the Bowman communications system, the costs and risks to the rival contracting teams in the long-preliminary stages (over six years), led them to come together, so collapsing the competition, with the MoD sacking the consortium and seeking new bids.

Sir Robert Walmsley, UK Defence Procurement Chief Executive, recognised that the Maritime Patrol Aircraft programme had presented a dilemma:

> It has taught me a lesson about competitions that are regarded as 'must wins', ie the company decides they just have to win and perhaps you get into a position where they almost want it too much because the consequences of the contract getting into trouble several years downstream, ghastly as they are, are far less ghastly than not getting the contract and wondering what you are going to do tomorrow (Bell M, 2000).

Government Information Technology projects financed under the Private Finance Initiative have experienced problems. A conference was told in November 1999 that there have been too many deals where there had been a 'stupid Dutch auction' in which the winner had been the one willing to accept the 'stupidest risk that the stupidest supplier would take on in the competition.' In future IT companies would be required to demonstrate to the Government that they could make a profit. Similar scenarios have been witnessed across other government departments and authorities engaged in a bid process, with the prospect of 'best value' or 'value for money' becoming 'poor value'. The answer must be that in deciding bids, in the defence sector or elsewhere, the government closely looks at quality, performance specifications, levels of acceptable risk and projections of profitability. Poor profitability or unrealistic targets and high levels of risk should warn government departments that they are not necessarily getting the best deal for the department or the taxpayer.

In the UK defence industry it is argued that the MoD now has a choice of five prime contractors, namely BAE Systems, GKN, Thomson-CSF, Raytheon and Lockheed Martin. However, as defence consolidation continues apace, this choice which provides competition amongst the primes is unlikely to last. What will the MoD do when there are only two or three global defence conglomerates, as many predict? And sooner than that, there may be just one supplier of British armoured vehicles, as there is already one major aerospace company capable of building a fighter. Would the MoD really turn its back on the last specialist producers of military hardware in Britain, and buy abroad? The reality is that while there is currently some choice in the defence sector, that choice is narrowing. The United States has accepted the logic of consolidation. In considering placing the order for its Joint Strike Aircraft, the loss of the programme is judged to be so catastrophic for either Boeing or Lockheed Martin, that the Pentagon is considering splitting production between the two, no matter who wins the design competition. The total value of the JSF programme is estimated at a colossal $220 billion. In such a scenario, is competition a realistic way to control costs in the defence industry of the future? The answer may partly lie in encouraging competition at the sub-prime level, below the level of the major systems integrators. In the future there may also be an increasing separation between platform producers and systems integrators, who may become increasingly detached from traditional industry. In time, software, communications and specialist design companies could become the next generation of systems integrators.

More immediately, competition should be built around the capabilities, competences and processes to deliver a system and maintain it over its life cycle, at the prime level and further down the supply chain. Building on the smart procurement 'whole life' flexible approach, there is a need to build-in high performance specifications, upgrades and maintenance costs. This means that the emphasis for future procurement should not necessarily be on initial cost competition, but capability and value for money over the long-term life of the project. Off-the-shelf costs can be deceptive, attractively priced for initial purchase, but with a sting in the tail as maintenance, servicing and upgrade costs are taken into account.

Currently there is no realistic prospect of Article 296 of the Treaty of Amsterdam that exempts the defence industry from European competition law being significantly modified or abolished to promote a Single Market in defence. A more integrated and open European defence market would benefit European industry, providing improved mutual access to domestic markets. Lowering barriers to free trade and competition within Europe could only stimulate cross-border trade within the EU. However, before this could happen there would need to be greater procurement harmonisation and shared technology development within Europe, and more open access to the important

US defence market. A European single market in defence would encourage specialisation, force the less competitive European defence companies to the wall, and open up the EU to aggressive US competition. The two countries most affected would be France and Britain. Europe has two principal defence markets, the UK and France, which account for 61 per cent of West European equipment procurement expenditure, and 79 per cent of R&D spending. The UK alone accounts for 36 per cent of procurement and 44 per cent of R&D expenditure. Under current conditions, British shipbuilding would disappear almost overnight. Whole sections of French state-controlled industry would be under threat. There is no indication that EU Member Governments are willing to expose their defence industries to the vagaries of the market, even given the UK's reputation as one of the most open defence markets in the world.

The EU's Commission is pressing for more competence in the defence sector field. Whilst this is broadly opposed by the British Government, the reality is that the Commission is increasingly an important player in competition generally, and defence mergers and acquisitions in particular. Baroness Symons, UK Defence Procurement Minister, speaking at a RUSI defence seminar on 13 April 2000, made it quite clear that the Commission's aspirations should not lead to more red tape from Brussels, threatening the expected competitive savings from smart procurement:

> the European Commission has specific aspirations in the European defence equipment market. An enhanced Commission role in the European defence equipment market might be said to hold both benefits and drawbacks for Member States in theory. Equally, it is by no means clear at present how these aspirations will be taken forward, or by whom… But let me say that I think there will have to be a lot of hard talking about developments of that nature. There are substantial concerns – not solely about the way in which the Commission may operate in this respect- but about any suggestion that the benefits of smart procurement – benefits we are starting to see delivered- may be compromised. We are in the business first and foremost of making procurement cheaper, faster, better – not more hedged about with rules, not more bureaucratic, not less competitive. We need to see real evidence that others understand this – not just European governments but, if they really want a role, the Commission too. This is not a point on which we in the UK can compromise – it is fundamental to our thinking. (www.mod.uk/speeches)

Nevertheless, the Commission is extremely active on the civil side of European industrial restructuring, and the UK government even waived its rights under Article 296, giving the Commission oversight of the Thomson-CSF/Racal acquisition. Although the reluctance to give the Commission a role in procurement is understandable in terms of national (and vested) interests, it is more widely accepted that European industrial restructuring, even if it involves defence companies, is an EU and Commission issue. In any event, with the spread of civil interests of some of the main defence companies (BAE, Rolls-Royce and EADS, for example), it is becoming more difficult to separate 'defence' and 'civil' companies. Some companies are moving away from the tag 'defence company', preferring to be known as 'systems integrators', or 'systems companies.'

The development of Transnational Defence Companies (TDCs) is making the concept of national security of supply a somewhat outmoded concept. The Framework Agreement signed in Farnborough on 27 July 2000 between the UK, France, Germany, Italy, Sweden and Spain frankly acknowledged as much: 'The Parties recognise that the likely consequences of industrial restructuring will be the creation of TDCs, possible abandonment of national industrial capacity and thus acceptance of mutual dependence.' The old days of ensuring security of supply by making sure the national industrial base was capable of equipping and supplying the British Armed Forces were long past. However, the MoD was determined to try to ensure that in the new inter-dependent world, the UK's European allies could be relied upon to supply essential material. The Framework Agreement provided a legal base to ensure that supplies would be delivered, through binding legal agreement and contracts, with clauses to prevent the obstruction of supplies. It was also agreed to expedite supplies in times of crisis or armed conflict, and that the signatories would have the right to retain certain defined strategic activities, assets and installations, or reconstitute a national key strategic activity if required. The latter clause may give some comfort to national governments, but the fact is that globalisation, consolidation and collaborative procurement projects are making security of supply dependent on transnational co-operation (MoD, 2000b).

The revision of armaments programmes in the years ahead can provide EU Member States with an opportunity to initiate a process of convergence between EU military doctrines. It makes sense to place orders only if there is agreement on the doctrine for using the arms in question. It is certainly the role of organisations like OCCAR and the embryonic EAA to debate the conditions of use of equipment to be developed jointly. In addition, EU Member States must discuss their defence doctrines with one another, with a view to establishing the broad lines on which the defence industry could develop the military equipment needed for the missions identified. The Petersberg tasks, incorporated in the Amsterdam Treaty, provide a useful starting point.

Military doctrines must also be explored in further depth, as they are the framework in which the European defence sector operates. EU Member States will only benefit from the economies of scale resulting from defence industry restructuring if they can procure common equipment. This means that it is necessary to avoid producing military equipment with different costly options. The EU will benefit from European defence rationalisation and consolidation if they can succeed in equipping their armed forces with effective equipment at optimum cost. Since it is the EU Member States who purchase the military equipment, it is they who have the primary responsibility for harmonising their needs if they wish to support and sustain the creation of strong European defence companies.

It is axiomatic that a strong European defence industry is necessary for an effective EU Common European Security and Defence Policy, and to strengthen the existing CFSP. A European defence technology base is also an obvious pre-requisite for a European Security and Defence Identity within NATO. As Tony Blair said in Aachen on 14 May 1999, the EU future defence role must include 'greater integration in the defence industry and procurement.'

Conclusions and policy recommendations

- The abolition of juste retour is crucial. Juste retour is extremely uncompetitive and inefficient. Establishing a European Armaments Agency by 2003 should be an EU priority. The benefits to the EU of backing an effective EAA, which rejected juste retour, would be significant.

- The WEU's WEAG and WEAO should be wound-up over the next three years, and their responsibilities folded into NATO, as the WEU effectively ceases to exist. OCCAR should be retained for the time being and form the model for the operation of the EAA, with the former eventually merging into the latter.

- OCCAR should in the meantime be awarded management of further substantial programmes (in addition to the A400M military airbus), to enhance its credibility and status as Europe's leading collaborative armaments organisation, for example Meteor and a future EuroTank project.

- The MoD should instigate a study of the effectiveness and the processes adopted in the smart procurement initiative, review progress so far, and consider any changes or improvements which might or might not be necessary.

- As consolidation and globalisation narrows the choice of prime contractor, competition in the UK and elsewhere should be particularly encouraged at the sub-prime level, below the level of the major systems integrators. Competition should be built around the capabilities, competences and processes to deliver a system and maintain it over its life cycle, at the prime level and further down the supply chain. Building on the smart procurement 'whole life' flexible approach, there is need to build-in high performance specifications, upgrades and maintenance costs. This means that the emphasis for future procurement should not necessarily be on initial cost competition, but on capability and value for money over the whole long-term life of the project.

- Before the European defence industry can consider participating in joint procurement, there must be political, military and strategic agreement on what is required when by Europe's armed forces. There is a need to agree on a strategic framework for the EU's new defence capabilities, and how they can meet the requirements of deployability and sustainability within the overall force structure. Exact equipment needs will have to be quantified on a multilateral basis, allowing for the principle of interoperability, both amongst the EU Member States and their non-EU NATO allies.

- The revision of armaments programmes in the years ahead can provide EU Member States with an opportunity to initiate a process of convergence between EU military doctrines. EU Member States must discuss their defence doctrines with one another, with a view to establishing the broad lines on which the defence sector could develop the military equipment needed for the missions identified. The Petersberg tasks provide a starting point.

- Military doctrines must be explored in further depth, as they are the framework in which the European defence sector operates.

V: Defence diversification, industrial strategy and innovation in the UK and regions

Defence diversification, innovation and the supply chain

The UK has no industrial strategy for the British defence industry. Such a statement is not particularly revelatory to those in the industry, and does not come as a surprise to policy analysts. After all, as Peter Robinson, senior economist at IPPR has shown, the government does not have a coherent regional policy either (Robinson, 2000). Establishing Regional Development Agencies (RDAs), and calling upon them all to grow faster than the national average is arithmetical nonsense and will hardly encourage sensible targeting of resources and a narrowing of regional disparities. Setting up the RDAs does not itself constitute a policy. According to some well-placed sources, there is in any event no significant regional concentration of the defence sector, so by implication there is no need for a regional policy to support them. Others in the industry argue that if the industry has survived up to now without an industrial strategy, why bother with one now? Somewhere in the middle of the debate sits the uncertain role of the under-resourced Defence Diversification Agency (DDA), created after five lines were inserted in Labour's 1997 election manifesto:

> Labour will establish a defence diversification agency so that where there is excess capacity due to shifting procurement needs, the skills of our defence workers are, wherever possible, retained for use in either alternative areas of the defence industry or in the civil manufacturing sector. The costs of the agency will be met from within existing MoD resources (Labour Party, 1997).

The creation of the DDA reflected the fact that while defence expenditure fell by almost a third between 1979 and 1997, the number of UK defence jobs almost halved, from 740,000 in 1980 to 360,000 in 1994.

The issue here is that while the Labour Government may have a policy towards the UK defence industry, it does not have a strategy. The Smart Procurement Initiative (SPI) represents one aspect of government policy, that is the desire to achieve value for money for the taxpayer in defence. More broadly, Labour's policy towards the defence industry is supportive, although short on specifics. As the Labour Party's 'Britain in the World' policy statement says:

> A strong and competitive defence industry is essential…We will therefore continue to promote efforts to restructure the European defence industry to enable it to compete effectively and collaborate from a position of strength with the new American giants. However, while government can play an important facilitating role, any restructuring must be industry-led.

The policy document was endorsed by the government Ministers and the Party conference in Brighton in September 2000. So, while the government will support, facilitate and promote restructuring, at the end of the day it is down to industry to compete effectively in the global market. The question is, can and should the government do more than exhort?

Of course there are agencies that do valuable work supporting the UK defence industry, such as the MoD's Defence Export Services Organisation (DESO) – see www.deso.mod.uk, the Defence Evaluation and Research Agency (DERA, about to be partly privatised) and the new Defence Diversification Agency (DDA). DERA is currently one of Europe's largest research organisations, with 12,000 staff and a turnover of about £1 billion, offering a range of services including operational studies and analysis, basic and applied research to consultancy advice and the test and evaluation of equipment. Under plans announced by the government, about three-quarters of DERA's activities would be privatised, but the most sensitive areas (including the chemical and biological defence sector at Porton Down), will be retained by the MoD. Some 9,000 staff would transfer to New DERA. DESO estimates it saves the MoD £400 million per year, through reduced fixed overhead charges resulting from the UK's £5 billion annual defence exports. DESO figures show that exports account for 40 per cent of defence output and 130,000 of the 455,000 defence industry jobs (see, for example, House of Commons, 1998 or www.dra.hmg.gb).

On the DDA, the National Policy Forum *Report to Conference* stated:

> And with the Defence Diversification Agency, established by Labour we will ensure that the expertise of the defence industry is extended to civilian use. In a second term we will look at ways of building on and extending the work of the Defence Diversification Agency.
>
> We are already working on the expansion of science parks linked to research establishments around the country, in order to spread more widely scientific and technological expertise. (National Policy Forum, 2000)

Casting aside the fact that 'spin-ins' from the civilian sector are now more important than 'spin-outs' from the defence sector, the DDA offers a real opportunity to devise a strategy to assist defence restructuring, support the defence industries in the regions and encourage innovation in cooperation with government departments and the sometimes directionless RDAs. The new RDAs have faced criticism in several parts of the country, with critics saying they are remote from business, are too bureaucratic, their plans are too vague, and their efforts to promote the regions have been too pedestrian. While this is obviously not true of all RDAs, the picture across the country appears mixed.

The Defence Diversification Agency (DDA) was launched with the publication of the government's White Paper on 5 November 1998, as part of a key initiative aimed at creating greater benefit from the nation's investment in research and development within DERA, the MoD's Defence and Evaluation and Research Agency. The DDA effectively started operating on 1 January 1999. The DDA encompasses a range of developments already under way at DERA sites, including dual-use technology centres, science parks and innovation centres. The DDA was intended to exploit defence technology for the purpose of wealth creation. Labour 's election manifesto stressed the party's support for a 'strong UK defence industry, which is a strategic part of our industrial base as well as our defence effort.' Labour believed that part of the defence industry's expertise could 'be extended to civilian use through a defence diversification agency.'

The DDA was set-up to ensure that small and medium enterprises (SMEs) had appropriate access to the technological knowledge and facilities that DERA possesses. In establishing the DDA, the Government believed that what was required was not funds for defence conversion to other activities, but the harnessing of defence technology and expertise more widely available for commercial exploitation. The DDA's main output was to be a significant increase in technology transfer from the defence to the civil sector and vice versa. DERA was already involved in technology transfer, and the intention was to give its activities in this field sharper focus and emphasis. A Defence Diversification Council was to be established, with members drawn predominantly from industry, but including the chief executive of DERA, and other representation from trade unions, local and central government.

The DDA was also to encourage the widest possible exploitation of military technology by companies which serve only commercial markets, providing knowledge of what is available, encouraging access to DERA laboratories, stimulating transfer of the MoD's Intellectual Property Rights (IPR) and seek partnership with companies for programmes of co-development and adaptation. The DDA has opened 10 offices around the UK (in Farnborough, Haslar, Malvern, Porton Down, Rosyth, Glasgow, Plymouth and Solihull, in Northern Ireland and Wales),with a total of 14 expected by the end of the current financial year. Technology Diversification Managers (TDMs) are based at the offices, responsible for working with local business support organisations to provide access to information and facilitating the transfer of defence technology. At Rosyth, the DDA office is located within a Business Innovation Centre (BIC) on the Rosyth Europarc, and the DDA is also involved in a BIC in Enfield. The Europarcs are funded by the EU Commission's Innovation Directorate, while the seven UK BICs are part of a European-wide innovation initiative. The DDA often locates its offices near DERA sites, but is also keen work in innovation centres or science parks where there is no DERA presence. The DDA works in partnership with Business Links, Training and Enterprise Councils (TECS), RDAs and local enterprise companies (details on www.dda.gov.uk/dda).

However, there are three problems with the DDA as currently constituted. Its £2 million annual budget is risible, it focuses on technology transfer (what happened to defence diversification?), and its future structure is uncertain. Taking the last first, the DDA as currently constituted is part of the MoD and comes under the wing of DERA. The DDA director reports to the DERA chief executive. Since DERA is being partly-privatised in a Public Private Partnership (PPP) arrangement, the inclusion of the DDA and its 22 staff (led by Professor Damien McDonnell) within the existing DERA framework will therefore be of an interim nature. The question is whether the DDA should join NewDERA or remain in the MoD's 'retained DERA.' Given the fact that it is mainly the most sensitive parts of DERA that are being retained, a solution could be for the DDA to join NewDERA with a semi-autonomous status.

It is clear that with the disappearance of the EU's Konver defence diversification programme, and with the era of heavy job losses in the leading defence manufacturers coming to an end or at least levelling off, there is less emphasis across Europe on large-scale defence diversification programmes. However, with the focus moving away from the entrenchment of the 1990s, analysts of the UK defence sector are gradually shifting their attention to the supply chain and the role and viability of the country's SMEs.

Increasingly, consolidated/aerospace prime contractors will be buying from an international supply base, offering world-class technology at best price and delivery times. The prime contractors will be looking to establish preferred supplier agreements with their sub-contractors, with the latter gaining long-term assured custom and participation in the design and development process, in return for progressively reducing costs. Prime contractors will be searching for new partners on a global scale, to reduce costs while at the same time maximising added value an improving production processes. By so doing, the primes will seek to secure sustainable competitive advantage through their supply chains. Second and third tier supply companies may have to rationalise, seek partners with similar business interests, or become part of a transnational structure. Survival will depend upon greater company investment, R&D, innovation, training and product upgrades.

The UK defence industry is catching up with other manufacturing industries in adopting 'post-Fordism', which includes flexible manufacturing, 'just-in-time' inventory practices and computer-integrated production. An analogy can be made between what has happened in the car manufacturing industry and what is likely to happen to companies in the defence industry supply chain. For example, major car manufacturers like Ford have sharply reduced the number of suppliers they use. In the six years to 1996, the number of suppliers at Ford Europe fell by 80 per cent to 300, while the revenue per supplier quadrupled. There is no indication that the defence and aerospace supply chain companies are aware of what is likely to hit them soon, with a profound impact on their survivability, local jobs and regional economies. Nor is there any hint that the government has a strategy to deal with these developments. The overall result of European and transatlantic consolidation will be the increased outsourcing of non-core manufacturing activities, greater globalisation of the industry, prime contractors working with suppliers to improve technical and managerial capabilities, and enhancing information flows and technical exchange with suppliers to improve joint problem solving. Primes will reduce the number of suppliers, working only with the best.

Little is known about the supply base of the defence industry. Some of the companies themselves are unaware of the final destination of their components, and may not even know they are supplying the defence industry. In the UK the main studies are those under the DTI/MoD 'Value of Defence to the Economy' programme conducted by the universities of York and the West of England, Bristol. Other university teams have carried out some research in this area (such as Cranfield and Cardiff), and the principal non-university studies have been carried out by the Society of British Aerospace Companies. The findings have highlighted a number of issues. First, there is the breadth and depth of the supply chain itself. For example, in a study of the Rolls-Royce military engines business in 1992, 16 product groups were identified in the first tier, and 30 plus in the lower tiers. The implication is that the supply base spreads across many industrial groups and localities. The defence industry is therefore not just significant to those areas where the major companies operate, but through the supply bases impacts on almost the whole of the UK. Research suggests the supply chain is a densely inter-woven matrix or network within which small changes in demand have a disproportionate effect on businesses as they reverberate through the network from company to company.

The evidence points to fewer suppliers of much higher quality and capability now being required by the primes, and that these are increasingly drawn from a wider, global geographic area. Such suppliers, once located and locked into the supply network, will be expected to adopt full partnership arrangements including risk and technology burden-sharing. Their vulnerability to any downturns in the defence market will increase, but if successful, their potential for growth and profitability will be enhanced. The offset arrangements entered into by prime contractors on international contracts may be of benefit to them, but not to their main suppliers, who see little or no return from overseas offset agreements. Middle tier companies may thus carry extra risk and responsibility, without the reward, leading to 'offset lean squeeze.' Some analysts are concerned this might ultimately suffocate vital middle tiers (Braddon, 2000).

Looking at the regional picture, there are obvious regional clusters of defence companies, and this is particularly apparent in the civil and military aerospace sector. It is estimated that there may be as many as 1,500 aerospace companies in the UK. There are marked clusters around London, the South East, the South West, the

Midlands, the North West, and parts of Scotland, Wales and Northern Ireland. In employment terms, the greatest concentrations are in the North West (17 per cent), the South West (17 per cent) and the South East (11 per cent). In terms of the supply chain, the South East (35 per cent), South West (18.9) and West Midlands (18.1) had the high concentrations of suppliers to the equipment sector. The West Midlands, East Midlands and North West accounted for larger proportions of the value of supplies to the sector. Yet there is no government strategy to support these regional clusters of defence and aerospace companies, and their local supply chains. Indeed, in some government departments, there is a refusal to accept that these regional defence industry clusters exist at all (SBAC, 1999a; SBAC, 1999b).

Prime contractors need a strong supply base to remain competitive, and even if they are seeking global solutions, they derive a commercial advantage from having a domestic option. The UK primes still have to come to terms with the issue of supply chain management, and support for their domestic networks. UK prime contractors should be encouraged to second staff to work in the DDA, especially on supply chain and innovation issues. A logical step to support the supply chain and UK SMEs in the defence sector is to establish an Innovation Fund. Technological transfer needs to be paid for, and an Innovation Fund would give SMEs financial assistance both to pay for new seeding innovation and achieve successful technological transfers. The Innovation Fund would thus provide a mechanism to assist technological transfer from the defence to the civil sector, and vice versa. The Government should provide the DDA with £10 million seed money for the Innovation Fund, which in partnership with financial institutions, could lead to an Innovation Fund worth an estimated £500 million. The Innovation Fund would operate on a commercial basis, attracting investment from UK financial institutions. The DTI should ring-fence some of its innovation funds for the DDA. Such an Innovation Fund would act as real driving force for defence diversification, giving substance to the DDA's aspiration of becoming 'a world class technology innovation brokerage service to implement Government policy on defence diversification.

Furthermore, the Government should give further thought to how it can better co-ordinate the work of innovation across government departments. Despite the Government's support for innovation, policy in this area is disjointed and spread across a number of different departments, notably the DTI, the MoD and the Cabinet Office. Frankly, there is little 'joined-up' government taking place in the crucial field of innovation. For example, the DTI White Paper on Science and Technology failed to mention the DDA. It is unclear whether an Innovation Minister in the DTI is sufficient to achieve cross-departmental co-operation on innovation.

There is currently no government strategy on support for the defence industrial base. There are, however a number of policies to assist the defence and aerospace sector, mainly located in the DTI and MoD. For example, the DTI provided £530 million repayable launch investment for the super jumbo airbus A3XX, creating 22,000 new jobs in Britain. The DTI works with the MoD on procurement issues, and provides advice to the MoD's equipment approval committee. The MoD assists with R&D support, especially through DERA, and with sales support through DESO. Of the UK's total £1.2 billion military R&D spending in 1999, the government spent £574 million. Total spending on civil R&D in the same year was £683 million. The DTI, working with the MoD, the DETR and the Cabinet Office, should draw up a framework strategy document on current and proposed future policies and programmes to support the UK defence industrial base, and the supply chain network. The DTI and MoD should also consider the means of funding more demonstrators in the defence industry, so supporting early development programmes. Failure to act could result in a supply chain meltdown, with resulting heavy job losses. The Ford and Rover crises indicated how quickly a local difficulty can potentially turn into a regional and national catastrophe for the UK industrial base.

The regions

The decision to establish Regional Development Agencies was taken by the New Labour Government in 1997, following the manifesto commitment to give more emphasis to regional development in England. The White Paper 'Building Partnerships for Prosperity' was launched in December 1997, and after a period of consultation, the Regional Development Agencies Act 1998 was passed by Parliament. Eight RDAs have been established nationwide. The UK defence and aerospace industry is distributed around most of the English regions, however, as noted above there are particular clusters of activity in the North West, East and West Midlands, South West and South East RDAs. There is also an aerospace cluster in Greater London.

Many firms in these clusters serve one or more of the defence majors, often located within the same RDA (although some cross RDA boundaries). Such companies benefit from a pool of local labour trained and used to working to the high standards required of the industry. There are often close links to regional centres of higher and further education, providing training and research skills. As globalisation reduces the total number of suppliers, those left are increasingly under pressure to reduce costs, increase the value of their products and become more risksharing. This may entail increased co-operation between firms in the same industry, or to finding partners with complementary skills inside the UK or abroad. It is therefore imperative that the UK, nationally and at a local level, provides a business environment that will retain existing investment and win new investments from other US and European companies. It is also necessary to encourage the dissemination of best practices in business systems, manufacturing processes and research co-operation.

The RDAs should recognise the contribution of defence prime contractors to the overall health of regionally located supply chains. Working with Government Offices in the regions and local authorities, the RDAs should draw up strategies to provide support for the sector's larger defence companies. The RDAs should also develop inter-regional approaches to support the defence sector supply chain.

RDAs should adopt transparent and nationally accessible policies towards training and research. Although regionally located research and training agencies are regional assets, RDAs should also recognise that agencies like DERA, the DDA and universities are also vital national assets, and adopt strategies that reflect both local and national priorities. RDAs should encourage the development of a single, coherent business support system within their region, so simplifying access and improving cost effectiveness.

Currently there are bewildering array of contact points for advice on European issues and funding. RDAs should create single points of contact for information on European business issues and helping with funding applications. This is particularly important for giving SMEs access to the EU Sixth Framework R&D programmes. RDAs should also improve access to high-level educational and training agencies. They could help the defence industry and supply chain companies (especially SMEs) through the encouragement of single point research and training support agencies.

RDAs should encourage the expansion or creation of regional trade associations or comparable bodies. Regional groups of this nature are often best placed to understand the needs of local firms, especially defence sector SMEs and supply companies, and put these in the context of a broader national strategy. Finally, RDAs located in regions of defence industry clusters should ensure that at least one member of the RDA's board has experience of the defence sector and its supply chain.

Presently, the Government makes no serious impact assessment of major defence procurement decisions, and how these might affect regional economies and the national industrial base. When the MoD makes a major procurement decision currently, the Treasury advises on value for money aspects, and the DTI advises on the implications for UK plc of the various bids, including job prospects and the maintenance of long-term industrial capability. However, the DTI only looks at procurement decisions valued at over £100 million, and relies on prime contractors to provide the information on the employment and other prospects. The DTI's written advice is then transmitted to the MoD's equipment approval committee, which handles procurement decisions. This approach should be reviewed. Every country takes the economic impact of any major procurement decision into account, before making a final decision. A major programme (for example Meteor, the A400M, or Eurofighter) has a significant bearing on the country's industrial base, and an extremely important role in job creation in the regions. The Government should be more thorough and open in taking these factors into account, and the MoD should, together with the DTI and DETR, embark on an industrial and regional impact assessment of any major UK government defence procurement decisions. A major defence procurement programme impact assessment should therefore be undertaken by a special cross-departmental body, comprising officials from the MoD, DTI and DETR, with support research specialists, as required. Initially, major defence procurement programme impact assessments would only occur in cases where the value of the contract exceeds £100 million, but this figure should be kept under review.

Conclusions and policy recommendations

- UK prime contractors should be encouraged to second staff to work in the Defence Diversification Agency (DDA), especially on supply chain and innovation issues.

- An Innovation Fund should be established to support the supply chain and SMEs in the defence sector. An Innovation Fund would give SMEs financial assistance both to pay for new seeding innovation and achieve successful technological transfers. The Innovation Fund would provide a mechanism to assist technological transfer from the defence to the civil sector, and vice versa.

- The Government should provide the DDA with £10 million seed money for the Innovation Fund, which in partnership with financial institutions, could lead to an Innovation Fund worth an estimated £500 million. The DTI should ring-fence some of its innovation funding for the DDA. Such an Innovation Fund would act as a real driving force for defence diversification, giving substance to the DDA's aspiration of becoming 'a world class technology innovation brokerage service to implement Government policy on defence diversification.'

- The Government should look at how better to co-ordinate the work of innovation across the DTI, MoD (DERA/DDA), the DETR and the Cabinet Office's Performance and Innovation unit.

- The DTI, working with the MoD, the DETR and the Cabinet Office, should draw up a framework strategy document on current and proposed future policies and programmes to support the UK defence industrial base, and the supply chain network. The DTI and MoD should also consider the means of funding more demonstrators in the defence industry, so supporting early development programmes.

- The RDAs should recognise the contribution of defence prime contractors to the overall health of regionally located supply chains. Working with Government Offices in the regions and local authorities, the RDAs should draw up strategies to provide support for the sector's larger defence companies, and exercise a stakeholder interest in these core companies. The RDAs should also develop inter-regional approaches to support the defence sector supply chain.

- RDAs should adopt transparent and nationally accessible policies towards training and research. RDAs should also recognise that agencies like DERA, the DDA and universities are also vital national assets, and adopt strategies that reflect national and local priorities. RDAs should encourage the development of a single, coherent business support system within the region, so simplifying access and improving cost effectiveness.

- RDAs should create single points of contact for information on European business issues and helping with funding applications. RDAs should also improve access to high level educational and training agencies. They could also help the defence industry and supply chain companies (especially SMEs) through the encouragement of single point research and training agencies.

- RDAs should encourage the expansion or creation of regional trade associations or comparable bodies. Regional groups of this nature are often best placed to understand the needs of local firms, especially defence sector SMEs and supply companies.

- RDAs located in regions of defence industry clusters should ensure that at least one member of the RDA's board has experience of the defence sector and its supply chain.

- The MoD should, together with the DTI and DETR, embark upon an industrial and regional impact assessment of any major UK government defence procurement decisions. A major defence procurement programme impact assessment should therefore be undertaken by a special cross-departmental body, comprising officials from the MoD, DTI and DETR, with support research specialists as required.

- Initially, major defence procurement programme impact assessments would only occur in cases where the value of the contract exceeds £100 million, but this figure should be kept under review.

VI: A new strategic goal for Europe

A holistic approach to EU defence

It is worth reiterating that in order to guarantee a secure world, there is more to security policy than the development of streamlined military structures and capable armed forces. The defence of democratic institutions, and human and civil rights (as witnessed recently in Serbia) are also part of the EU's armoury to prevent and resolve conflicts. Environmental degradation, the proliferation of weapons of mass destruction, the growth of ethnic nationalism, international terrorism, crime and the traffic in drugs and people, all threaten global stability. Other important sources of insecurity include extreme economic deprivation, poverty and the marginalisation of social groups, which can give rise to fear, intolerance and conflict. While the short-term threat of global war has receded, regional and ethnic conflicts have escalated. The Gulf War, Bosnia, Croatia, Kosovo, Rwanda, the Congo, East Timor and Sierra Leone are just some of the more recent examples.

The EU, when approaching the issue of European defence, must embrace an enlarged notion of security which is defined in military and human terms. More emphasis should be placed on the role of foreign and development policy in security. In UK domestic terms, there should be a more holistic approach to security policy, with 'joined-up' policy co-ordination between the Foreign Office, MoD and the Department for International Development (DFID), so painfully absent in the Mozambique floods crisis, when an unseemly row broke out between the MoD and DFID over the cost of the relief operation. Labour recognises that existing definitions of security are inadequate, as the National Policy Forum report makes clear:

> Labour believes that we need a broader definition of security and, hence a more integrated approach to defence and international policy to respond to these crosscutting challenges. Military preparedness will remain essential. Just as important, however, are the promotion of democracy and good governance, human rights and the rule of law, and economic growth through sustainable development (National Policy Forum 2000)

As, UN Secretary-General Kofi Annan put it: 'The prevention of conflict begins and ends with the promotion of human security and human development.' Labour also accepted that it had to do more than just react to crises, it also had to do all it could to prevent conflicts happening in the first place. International diplomacy, aid, trade, investment and debt relief could all play a part, as could the concept of 'defence diplomacy' developed by former UK Defence Secretary George Robertson. Defence diplomacy is about building bridges with new allies and partners (especially in the Warsaw Pact), assisting the development of democratically accountable armed forces through new education and training initiatives, and facilitating security sector reform.

The importance of policy coherence between the Common Foreign and Security Policy (CFSP) and development policy should not be underestimated. In order to achieve a more meaningful definition of security, it is important to stress the necessity of ensuring coherence across First and Second pillar activities (that is broader Community actions/policy and the CFSP). Apart from the military aspects of security, the EU should also focus on the achievement of human security development issues. Conflict is at the heart of much human suffering and we should emphasise the need for the EU to tackle the root causes of conflict if human security is to be achieved. This would require a more coherent approach across all EU activities, and those of the 15 Member States. One way to help to develop this would be through the introduction of conflict impact assessments carried out by the Policy Planning and Early Warning Unit (PPU) established by the Amsterdam Treaty.

The PPU could assess how EU foreign, development, trade military and arms export policies are impacting on vulnerable countries. This would ensure that the EU, and its 15 Member States, avoid pursuing conflicting policies that only serve to exacerbate tensions and fuel instability. The EU's Development Council noted the importance of such a holistic approach when it recommended back in December 1998 that 'relevant experts' should examine the impact of the development policies of the Community and its Member States on peace and stability in developing countries.

A new strategic security goal for the EU

NATO will remain the main focus of the collective defence effort for Europe in the years ahead, as well as the focal point for transatlantic security co-operation. Today, all the major EU countries are engaged in a defence planning cycle that will take them up to 2015. Over the next few years (possibly by 2004-5) at least six countries could be new members of the EU, namely Cyprus, the Czech republic, Estonia, Hungary, Poland and Slovenia. These countries will bring the EU into direct contact with the unstable regions of Europe. Twenty-eight countries could in theory take part in EU-led military crisis management operations.

The Cologne and Helsinki European Councils established the EU's Political and Security Committee (PSC) and the Military Committee (MC), and a new Military Staff (MS) to support the work of the two committees. Javier Solana was appointed High Representative of the CFSP, Secretary General of the Council and Secretary of the Western European Union (WEU), to co-ordinate policy in this area. However, the institutional relationship between the Council's 'high representative' and the Commissioner for External Affairs (currently Chris Patten), who also speaks on the CFSP, is not working. The two roles overlap and duplicate each other. With the evolution of the Council as the dominant EU institution, the role of the High Representative and the Council should be paramount. The High Representative should be the primary international spokesperson for the CFSP and CESDP on behalf of the EU institutions. The High Representative's status should be boosted by being made permanent chair of the PSC, as well as chair of the General Affairs Council (which brings together EU foreign ministers). The rotating presidency, which confuses those outside the EU and adversely affects policy continuity, should also be abolished. The EU Commissioner for External Affairs and his/her directorate should act in an advisory role to the High Representative, acting rather like a Permanent Secretary in the British civil service, preparing options and implementing agreed Council policy on the CFSP.

The role of the Council itself should enhanced with regard to the CFSP and CESDP, with the secretariat under the High Representative and Secretary General of the Council preparing a draft annual agenda (to be ratified by the European Council). In addition to the General Affairs Council, a separate Defence Council should be established, to which EU defence ministers would be invited to discuss CESDP issues. The High Representative could also chair the Defence Council. Other Council sessions (such as the Agricultural Council) would be chaired by a Minister elected by their peers for an annual fixed term. European Council sessions would be prepared by an expanded Council Secretariat, working on an agreed annual agenda, but chaired on a rotating basis. The European Council, bringing together all the Heads of Government, should be the body which sets the political and economic agenda for Europe. However, the Commission would retain the power of initiative, bringing proposals to the European Council to implement the agreed annual agenda, which the latter could then discuss, amend and ratify. European Councils currently meet every three months. As Tony Blair outlined in his speech in Warsaw on 6 October 2000, such a structure would not be intended to undermine the role of the Commission:

> The President of the Commission is a member of the European Council, and would play his full part in drawing up the agenda. He would then bring a proposal for Heads of Government to debate, modify and endorse. It would be a clear legislative, as well as political, programme setting the workload of individual Councils. The Commission's independence as guardians of the treaty would be unchanged. And the Commission would still bring forward additional proposals where its role as guardian of those treaties so required. But we would have clear political direction, a programme and a timetable by which all the institutions would be guided (see www.fco.gov.uk/news/speechtext).

Nevertheless, the Commission was clearly witnessing a shift in the balance of power in the EU institutions, away from itself and towards the European Council and individual governments. Since the glory days of Jacques Delors, the Commission has seen its power and influence decline, reaching its nadir at the time of the resignation of Jacques Santer's Commission in 1999. Santer's demise showed how the Commission was even losing ground to the European Parliament, as MEPs forced the Commission to resign over allegations of mismanagement and sleaze. The European Commission's positive response to Tony Blair's speech underlined the desire of Romano Prodi and his Commissioners' to regain lost authority, and respond to a call to give direction to the EU's institutions.

The EU needs to establish a New Strategic Security Goal (NSSG) which looks beyond the Headline Goal set at the Helsinki Summit. The EU must decide now what its security goals are for the medium to long-term, beyond 2003. The public should also be informed about the EU's purpose in seeking to establish a CESDP (the 'end game'). The NSSG should fulfil three criteria: political legitimacy, military capability and affordability. By 2015, EU forces (including the European Rapid Reaction Force) should able to carry out a Kosovo-type operation without recourse to US military assets. Such a capability will require a range of core elements:

- a common threat perception
- an institutional structure that can manage all aspects of crises (military and civil)
- a 'shadow' defence planning structure that, whilst using the same doctrine as NATO, would enable autonomous EU action

- a new holistic security concept that is defined in military and non-military, human terms
- civilian and military crisis management capabilities
- autonomous assets in areas such as strategic intelligence, strategic and tactical lift and logistics
- secure supply and re-supply of military equipment
- a common operational budget (Algeri, 2000).

As with the ERRF created by Helsinki, the forces available to the EU will also have to be answerable to other force structures, like NATO. There will be very few new pools of forces available to the EU. While NATO remains the cornerstone of European defence over the next thirty years, the EU should plan for the possibility that the US reduces its military personnel presence on the continent significantly (say by about half to 50,000, including the Sixth Fleet), retaining only a 'rapid reinforcement' capability.

EU-NATO relations and institutional links also need to be established on a sound footing. Instead of the current *ad hoc* arrangements, an EU-NATO Consultation Council should be created. The Consultation Council would form an operational institutional link between the Council, Commission and NATO. DSACEUR, NATO's Deputy Supreme Allied Commander (who is always a European) responsible for the European Rapid Reaction Force, must sit on the EU's Military Committee as of right, and be invited to Council meetings of EU foreign and defence ministers which discuss the CESDP. The 'toolbox paper', agreed as a basis for further discussion between the EU 15 accepted only that DSACEUR should 'normally participate' as appropriate in meetings of the Military Committee. Double-hatting of military representatives to NATO and the EU should be agreed standard practice. Out of the 15 Member States, 13 are presently double-hatted to NATO and the EU through their Military Representatives or military Heads of Mission. This practice should be extended to all the EU 15.

In order to ensure long-term operational autonomy for the EU, a certain degree of duplication of NATO assets and structures will be inevitable, although these should be minimised wherever possible. The relevant areas are likely to include strategic intelligence, advanced communications, tactical surveillance and reconnaissance, strategic and tactical lift and logistics. The EU should embark upon a long-term study on likely requirements within a fifteen-year and thirty-year planning cycle, including sources of supply, specifications and funding.

Over the period 2000-2015, the EU would gradually increase its operational effectiveness so that by 2015 the European Union would be capable of almost all collective security missions, including:

- peacetime emergency evacuation of European citizens, counter-crime and counter-drugs
- defence diplomacy to build trust, dispel hostility and assist in the development and promotion of democratically accountable armed forces
- peace support and humanitarian operations, operations other than war in support of European interests, international peacekeeping/peacemaking and humanitarian principles
- conflict prevention, economic security and diplomatic measures/actions
- regional conflict outside the EU which could affect European security, interests or international security
- regional conflict inside the EU, involving a request for assistance from an EU Member State.

The progressive expansion of EU tasks and missions would be accompanied by increasing professionalisation of European forces, and the creation of larger pools of highly-trained and well-equipped troops.

By 2015, the EU would be able to provide substantial force packages for peacekeeping/peacemaking operations, within or outside the EU. However, already by 2003, the EU should make available the ERRF, or elements of the rapid reaction force, for peacekeeping/peacemaking operations either in or outside the EU, under UN or other auspices. Reform of the UN's role in peacekeeping and conflict prevention will be vital in ensuring that the EU can collectively and effectively participate in United Nations' peacekeeping operations. The UN will have to ensure that in future, it has at its disposal professional and properly trained troops, acting under a robust mandate and rules of engagement, backed up by a permanent peacekeeping high command. The UN has to face the fact that peacekeeping operations may often resemble war, with Peace Enforcement (PE) designed to fill the gap between peacekeeping and war. The UN would also have to establish a clear framework for UN humanitarian intervention, even where there might be a threat of a veto in the Security Council.

Some advances have been made on all these fronts. The UN itself has produced a critical report on the weakness of present peacekeeping operations, produced by a panel chaired by Lakhdar Brahimi, Algeria's former foreign minister. The US has endorsed proposals to establish a permanent peacekeeping high command to replace the existing and cumbersome ad hoc arrangement. Robin Cook, UK Foreign Secretary, has also produced some suggested reforms to strengthen the Security Council and the UN's peacekeeping role. To broaden membership of the Security Council, Robin Cook has proposed adding five new members (Germany, Japan and one each from Africa, Asia and Latin America), to the existing post-war P5 (Britain,

France, the US, Russia and China). He also suggests four new non-permanent members, to make the Security Council more representative of the international community. More contentiously, the Foreign Secretary outlined six principles to guide humanitarian intervention, even when opposed by the state concerned, and not backed by unanimity in the Security Council (as was the case in Kosovo):

- more concentration on conflict prevention
- the use of armed force should only be a last resort
- responsibility in the first place lies with the state where severe violations are taking place
- when a government has shown that it is unwilling or unable to cope with a humanitarian catastrophe, the international community has a responsibility to intervene
- any use of force should be proportionate to achieving the humanitarian purposes of the mission and carried out in accordance with international law
- the use of force must be collective and only in exceptional circumstances should it be undertaken without the express authority of the Security Council of the UN.
- a full economic, social and political programme to secure peace and stability must also accompany intervention.

The only issue here is that the above guidelines would almost certainly justify intervention in Chechnya (at the height of the conflict), and possibly even Tibet. Both interventions would be ruled out as impractical, politically unacceptable, militarily hazardous and possibly globally destabilising. Yet, the fact that intervention is ruled out in some cases does not mean that the UN could not and should not act where it can prevent a humanitarian catastrophe, and promote or restore democracy.

Robin Cook also suggested creating more robust rules of engagement, a UN military inspectorate general, and a UN military staff college. On the latter, the British Foreign Secretary wrote that the staff college would 'train forces for the UN in peacekeeping. We would be happy for the UN to establish such a college in the UK' (see www.fco.gov.uk/news/speechtext). The UK government's offer to the UN is very significant. It not only shows the Government's commitment to UN peacekeeping operations, but provides a unique opportunity to link the peacekeeping/peacemaking role envisaged for the EU under the Petersberg tasks, with the proposed UK-based UN military staff college. If the UK government's offer to establish the UN military staff college is accepted, the staff college should also offer training and courses in peacekeeping/peacemaking to European military personnel, with particular emphasis on the Petersberg tasks. The UN military staff college would also have the advantage of being open to all nationalities and military personnel interested in developing peacekeeping skills, including non-European members of NATO, and partner states like the Ukraine and Russia. In any event, the emphasis given to UN peacekeeping operations by the Labour government foreshadows a more pro-active role for European forces in future peacekeeping/peacemaking operations both on the continent and beyond.

To complement the UK's UN peacekeeping initiative and the proposed UN military staff college, a new peacekeeping doctrine for all EU forces is needed. The integration of national elements into a European multinational force raises a number of specific issues, such as doctrine, command language, joint training, objectives, acceptable levels of risk, attitudes to local populations, rules of engagement and the use of force. A European Combined Joint Staff College (ECJSC), building on the Eurocorps experience, would be a useful mechanism for addressing these issues. The ECJSC should be established by 2003 to plan for EU Peace Support Operations (PSOs), and to work on issues surrounding the role of the European Rapid Reaction Force in support of Petersberg tasks. The ECJSC should complement, and not duplicate the work of the UN military staff college, with the latter concentrating on the broader issues of UN peacekeeping operations.

The EU needs to undertake a European Strategic Defence Review (ESDR), to be completed by 2003. An ESDR would define the missions, structures capabilities and resources needed for European forces and act as the core planning framework. The ESDR would review the role of a CESDP in areas such as peacetime security, European defence diplomacy, wider European interests, regional conflicts, and peace support and humanitarian operation inside and outside the EU. Such an ESDR cannot be conducted from within NATO, which has a different role. After 2003, the missions of EU military forces should be broadened and military tasks increased, so that progressively more ambitious operations can be undertaken. The expansion of missions and tasks will be linked to the progressive professionalisation of European armed forces. The ESDR should be repeated every three years, to match missions with tasks.

The ESDR could also act as a focal point for a public information campaign, to reinforce popular support for developments in EU defence. The UK's 1998 SDR could serve as a model, combining public consultation with a broad dissemination of information. As part of the ESDR, a Europe-wide study should be undertaken to look at the implications of the Revolution in Military Affairs (RMA) for European forces, the possible advantages of RMA, specific programmes and likely costs.

At the heart of European defence planning should be a European Combined Joint Task Force, that is an EU Permanent Military Headquarters onto which European national forces can 'bolt-on'. In addition to EU duties, the Headquarters would co-ordinate operational planning and act as the operations planning link with NATO. Building on the WEU audit of 1999, the EU needs to establish specific command, control, communications and computer systems for autonomous operations, based on a study of existing assets, planned assets and shortfalls.

Further satellite intelligence capabilities are required in addition to the two Helios 1 satellites (owned by France, Italy and Spain) and designated military satellite communication systems, to avoid dependence on the United States. France's annual Helios budget amounts to some Euro: 150 to 200 million, although the optical satellites have been criticised for performing badly in poor weather. However, as these satellites are so expensive, and EU Member States may not be able to afford them and meet their strategic capability goals, the EU should examine what further use can be made of the improving Commercial Satellite Imagery (CSI) for Peace Support Operations (PSOs). The WEU's Satellite Centre at Torrejon in Spain should be transferred to the EU, and it should develop its capacity to analyse photographs from commercial satellites. Although the British enjoy a privileged security arrangement with the United States, gaining access to data from US satellites, there is concern in other European countries (particularly France) that US intelligence may not always be freely supplied to America's European allies. There have even been accusations of the US deliberately supplying low grade or misleading intelligence, and even with the UK, Britain experienced limited help from US satellite intelligence in the first month of the Falklands war in 1982.

The EU should also develop autonomous capabilities in the field of aerial reconnaissance, which is a less expensive option than developing satellites. Unmanned aerial vehicles (UAVs) took some better photographs in Kosovo than some spy satellites. The EU should pool their UAV programmes to create an autonomous capability, providing battlefield intelligence to its forces. On the intelligence front, the EU should also establish an EU-level Joint Intelligence Committee (EJIC), along the lines of the UK's JIC, made of senior intelligence figures from each member state. The European Joint Intelligence Committee should share intelligence with the US and NATO, on a reciprocal basis.

In addition to the planned enhancement of a strategic lift capability, the EU should create a European air transport command (Eurolift), as proposed at the Helsinki European Council. Such a command, involving joint logistics, training and maintenance, would improve military efficiency and provide cost savings. Eurolift could also be extended to sea transport and air-to-air refuelling (see also chapter 1).

Geoff Hoon, UK Defence Secretary, has said that the WEU is reaching 'the end of its sensible working life.' Decisions still have to be taken about the WEU's residual functions which may remain as the organisation is wound up. Several suggestions have already been made about the WEAO, WEAG, and the Torrejon Satellite Centre. Some of the WEU's functions are being transferred to the EU, some could go to NATO, while others are discarded. For example, the 1948 Modified Brussels Treaty and the Article 5 collective defence guarantee it includes for full members could remain, but should continue to be met through NATO, where each nation has a complimentary commitment.

The expertise of the WEU Institute for Security Studies should not be lost. The WEU Institute should be converted into an EU Institute for Security Studies. The EU Institute for Security Studies would become a centre supporting the command and planning elements of the EU, with academic and policy expertise.

There remains the question of what to do about the WEU Parliamentary Assembly, which was founded in 1954. The Assembly consists of 115 parliamentarians from the 10 WEU full Member States; 20 members from the associate members of Iceland, Norway and Turkey; 34 members from the associate partners of Estonia, Latvia, Lithuania, Bulgaria, the Czech Republic, Hungary, Poland, Romania, Slovakia and Slovenia; and 20 members from the observer states of Austria, Denmark, Finland, Ireland and Sweden. The WEU Assembly, meeting in special session in Lisbon on 21 March 2000, called for itself to be transformed into a CESDP Assembly. Another suggestion, from the UK's House of Commons Defence Select Committee, has been to set up a parliamentary body along the lines of COFAC (the EU-based Conference of Foreign Affairs Committees), which allows participation by countries aspiring to join the EU. This could provide a forum for the defence committees of the Member States' parliaments, possibly working with COFAC, to have a structured exchange of views on the CESDP, involving existing and aspirant EU and NATO members.

As the House of Commons Defence Select Committee reported:

> The setting-up of the CESDP means that the democratic deficit in holding the Council of Ministers to account for actions taken under the provisions of the 'second pillar' of the EU has become more apparent and the finding of a solution more urgent. Any proposal to remedy this must recognise the intergovernmental nature of the pillar's arrangements by emphasising the role of national parliaments (House of Commons 2000).

Prime Minister Tony Blair has entered the debate parliamentary oversight of the CESDP, given the intention to abolish the WEU Assembly. Tony Blair's proposed solution is to create a second chamber of the European Parliament, which would 'help provide democratic oversight of the common foreign and security policy.' Because of the inter-governmental nature of defence, Member States are unwilling to cede these powers to the supranational European Parliament and its existing MEPs. Speaking in Warsaw in October 2000, the Prime Minister made it clear that the second chamber would not get involved in the 'day-to-day negotiation of legislation.' The second chamber would have a reviewing function, ensuring the principle of subsidiarity, so that EU decisions were devolved to the relevant national or local level where appropriate. The Blair formula is more ambitious than the Defence Select Committee's option, involving national parliamentarians at a deeper institutional level in the work of the EU, and attempting to reconnect the 'remote' EU institutions with the European voting public. Directly elected as the European Parliament is, falling turn-outs (23 per cent in the UK in 1999) and voter disenchantment with the EU's institutions have raised the spectre of strengthening the political legitimacy of the European Union's structures. However, to revitalise the political legitimacy of EU's institutions and provide parliamentary accountability for the CESDP, while embracing non-EU European countries, more will have to be done than sending a few national MPs from the EU 15 to a second chamber. The WEU Assembly's call for yet another parliamentary assembly (in addition to the OSCE Parliamentary Assembly, the Council of Europe and the North Atlantic Assembly), appears doomed to failure on grounds of cost and unnecessary duplication. The proposed WEU 'European Security and Defence Assembly' would effectively be a reborn WEU Assembly.

By 2002, the EU should establish a senate, or second chamber of the European Parliament consisting of national parliamentarians nominated from the EU Member States, associate members, partners and observers of the former WEU Assembly, which should be abolished. Only parliamentarians from existing EU member States would have full voting rights, all the others should attend as speaking but non-voting observers. The senate would ensure parliamentary accountability over the CESDP. On appropriate occasions, observers from the Russian Federation and the Ukraine should also be invited to by the President or Senate Speaker to sessions on the CESDP (to speak but not vote). It is important that the European Parliament's senate does not exclude those countries which previously had rights to attend the WEU, and debate and report on European security issues. The senate should have its own secretariat, building on the strengths of the WEU Assembly administration.

However, the European Parliament should not become a bloated bureaucracy, costing the taxpayers of Europe even more money. It has been agreed to cap the European Parliament's number of MEPs at a ceiling of 700. With the creation of a senate of 200 national MPs including observers, the ceiling for the number of MEPs in the first chamber should be cut to 500, from a current total of 626. The 500 MEPs in the first chamber should include MEPs from the 13 applicant states, with the figure being revised on the successful accession of the 13th new Member State. This will require a reduction in national MEP quotas at the time of the accession of the first wave of new EU Member States (possibly in 2004), but will save the European taxpayers money. National MPs in the senate should be paid national parliamentary delegation rates for attendance at the European Parliament, in line with current WEU Assembly payments. The overall effect of the proposed reforms should be a net saving to the European taxpayer. These savings would be higher if France could be persuaded to shift the parliament permanently from Strasbourg to Brussels, instead of parliamentarians commuting between the two institutions (at an additional cost of £100 million per annum).

Moving towards common defence

The EU's new Strategic Security Goal will have two phases, covering from 2000-2015, and from 2015 to 2030. The second phase involves the progressive transfer of military decision-making, command and control competences into a single structure, while retaining the political inter-governmental decision making to heads of government at a political level. No troops would ever be committed to any security operation without the consent of their government.

In particular, phase two would see a move away from purely collective security and force projection towards collective defence and ultimately common defence. Over a thirty year planning framework, the EU should undertake work to examine the force levels necessary to protect the European home base from every type of threat, and fight a Major Theatre War (MTW). These developments would suggest a move away from task-sharing in the medium to long-term towards specialisation (especially in logistics), and the emergence of common supranational 'groupements' that replace national units such as regiments and divisions. Specialisation is always under way to some degree. The UK for example can still field full or part formations as part of NATO task-sharing, but has less capabilities than the French or Germans in areas such as air defence and armour. It is thus necessary for the EU to move from a combined and joint approach to the establishment of common force packages and elements. This would not mean the creation of a European standing army, but multinational force packages. Planning would have to begin almost immediately, as much military equipment has a 30 to 40-year lifespan.

To avoid the marginalisation and isolation of the Russian Federation and the Ukraine, both these countries should be candidates to join NATO by 2030. NATO should invite the Russian Federation and the Ukraine to join its Membership Action Plan (MAP), building on the Partnership for Peace (PfP) initiative, with a view to being full candidates for NATO membership by 2030. The Russian Federation does not regard the NATO-Russia Founding Act and Permanent Joint Council as a satisfactory model for fully involving Moscow in the evolving European security architecture and the expanding NATO. There is a danger that as NATO enlarges to the east (beyond Poland, Hungary and the Czech Republic), and the EU enhances its defence capabilities (and enlarges to the Balkans and east), Russia will be increasingly alarmed that its own security and vital interests are threatened. This is particularly the case with the Baltic States wishing to join NATO as soon as possible (the Estonian border is 150 kilometres from St Petersburg). To allay these fears, and to avert a drift away from democracy and towards anti-westernism in Russia, the EU and NATO should involve Moscow in Europe's evolving security architecture. On a political level, Russian representatives could be invited to the European Parliament's new senate to discuss relevant security issues on an occasional basis, whilst NATO shows that is not in any way aimed against Moscow by extending the prospect of membership, albeit in the long-term. To underpin democracy and

Ukrainian independence, the same offer of political engagement and possible future NATO membership should also be made to Kiev.

By 2030, NATO's US presence on the continent will have been reduced to several key air bases, headquarters staff and skeleton ground-force bases with rapid reinforcement capability, and a strong presence in the Mediterranean with the Sixth Fleet. Whilst NATO remains the cornerstone of European defence in all-out war, by 2015 the EU will be capable of carrying out Petersberg task peacekeeping/peacemaking operations on the continent and beyond. In addition, by 2030 the EU will also have developed the capabilities to mount a common defence in the face of any threat to European security.

The Amsterdam Treaty spoke of 'the progressive framing of a common defence policy...which might lead to a common defence, should the European Council so decide.' The new Strategic Security Goal for the EU should be to achieve a European common defence by 2030.

Select bibliography

Adams, G et al (1999) *Europe's Defence Industry: a transatlantic future?* London: CER

Adams, G (2000) 'Convergence or Divergence?: the Future of the Transatlantic Defense Industry', Elliott School of International Affairs, Washington DC: The George Washington University

Algeri, F, Hauser, A, Lindley-French, J (2000) 'Enhancing the European Union as an International Security Actor', Gutersloh: Bertelsmann Foundation Publishers.

Ashborne, A (2000) 'Open the US defence market', *CER Bulletin*, Issue 10, February/March

Beaver, P (2000) 'In Step with the Forces?', Parliamentary Monitor, Vol 8, no. 10, September

Bell, M (2000) *Leaving Portsoken: defence procurement in the 1980s and 1990s*, London: BAE Systems

Bereuter, D (2000) US House of Representatives, 'Outline of American (US) Perspective on the Creation of the ESDI Within the European Union', Washington DC, 16 March

Bertram, C, Grant, C and Heisbourg, F (2000) 'European defence: the next steps', *CER Bulletin*, Issue 14, October/November

Blair, T (1998) 'It's time to repay America' in the New York Times on 13 November

Bole-Richard, M (1999) 'L'Italie met fin au service militaire obligatoire' *Le Monde*, 5-6 September

Braddon, D (2000) 'Restructuring the European Defence Industry: Supply Chain Issues', unpublished

Bridge, T (1998), 'Modern Forces for the Modern World: The SDR promises much', *Army Quarterly and Defence Journal*, Vol 128, no.3, July edition

Broome, S and Field P (1999) UK Research Partnership Ltd, 'SBAC Supply Chain Research project: Phase One Report, London: Society of British Aerospace Companies

Cevasco, F (2000) *Defense Science Board Task Force on Globalization and Security-Summary Briefing*, Hicks and Associates Inc, Washington DC, February

Cook, P (1999) *An uncertain future for Central European defence industries*, Brussels: International Security Information Service

Defense Science Board (DSB) Task Force on Globalization and Security (1999), Final Report, December, Washington DC: Office of the Under Secretary of Defense for Acquisition and Technology

Edgecliffe, A and Parkes, C (2000) 'BAe in $1.6bn US purchase', *Financial Times*, 14 July

European Council Cologne, (1999) *Conclusions of the Presidency*, 3-4 June 1999

European Council, Helsinki (1999) *Conclusions of the Presidency*, 10-11 December 1999 Community document no. 20699

European Council, Santa Maria da Feira, (2000) *Conclusions of the Presidency*, 19-20 June 2000

European Parliament, Sub-Committee on Security and Disarmament (1998), PE 228.752; *Text of the French-British European defence statement Saint-Malo (France)- 4 December 1998*

French Defence Ministry (1999) *Les enseignements du Kosovo*, November

Garden T and Roper, J (1999) 'Pooling Forces', *CER Bulletin*, December edition

Gnesotto, N (2000) 'Transatlantic debates', *Newsletter*, No 23, April, Paris: WEU Institute for Security Studies

Grant, C (1999) 'Transatlantic alliances and the revolution in military affairs', in *Europe's defence industry: a transatlantic future?* London: CER

Grant, C (2000) 'Intimate relations: can Britain still play a leading role in European defence – and keep its special links to US intelligence?', London: Centre for European Reform

Grant, C (2000) 'EU 2010: an optimistic vision of the future', London: CER

Grant, R (2000) 'The RMA- Europe can keep in step', *Occasional Papers 15*, June, Paris: WEU Institute for Security Studies

Harnischfeger, U (1999) 'DaimlerChrysler attacks BAe deal', *Financial Times*, 18 March

Hatfield, R (2000) 'NATO's new strategic concept', *Defence Systems Daily*, 26 January

Hawkey, E and Little, N (1998) 'Insurance Policy' *Defence Review*, Autumn edition

Hawkey, E and Winfield, G (1999) 'Not flying the flag', *Defence Review*, Summer edition

Hayward, K (1999) 'Global Rationalisation and the UK Aerospace Industry, London: Society of British Aerospace Companies

Hayward, K (1999) 'UK Aerospace and the Regions: a national industry with a regional impact', London: SBAC

Hayward, K (2000) 'Globalisation, the revolution in Military Affairs and the Future of the World Defence Industrial System', London: Society of British Aerospace Companies

Heisbourg, Francois (1999) 'The EU needs defence convergence criteria', *CER Bulletin*, Issue 6, June/July

House of Commons (1998) Defence Select Committee, Sixth Report, 'The Defence Evaluation and Research Agency', July

House of Commons (2000) Defence Select Committee, Eighth Report, on European Security and Defence (HC 264) Session 1999-2000,

Institute for Strategic Studies (1999) 'The Military Balance 1999-2000', Oxford: Oxford University Press

Institute for Strategic Studies (2000) 'Strategic Survey 1999-2000' Oxford: Oxford University Press

Kettle, M (2000) 'Bush adviser warns Europe to spend more on arms', *The Guardian*, 7 June

Labour Party (1997) *New Labour: Because Britain Deserves Better* (Manifesto) Labour Party

Lutz, Brigadier General Ernst (2000) 'Germany's Strategic Choices', *RUSI Journal*, April

Maguire R and Gow D (2000) 'Buy our arms, pleads Clinton *Guardian* 17 February

Mathiopoulos, M and Gyarmati, I (1999), 'Saint Malo and Beyond: Toward European Defence', *The Washington Quarterly*, Autumn edition

Mey, H (1998) 'The Revolution in Military Affairs: A German Persepective', *Comparative Strategy*, July-September

Ministry of Defence (2000a) *Strategic Defence Review: Modern Forces for the Modern World*, MoD

Ministry of Defence, (2000b) 'Treaty Signed Supporting the Restructuring of the European Defence Industry', www.mod.uk, 27 July

Morgan, O (2000) 'Blair in £900m missile row' *Observer* 27 February

National Policy Forum (2000) Report to conference, Conference 2000, Brighton, 24-28 September

NATO Summit Declaration, (1999a) S(99)63, 23 April 1999

NATO (1999b) Defence Capabilities Initiative', NAC-S(99)69, press release, 24 April 1999

Naumann, Klaus (2000) 'Europe's military ambitions', *CER Bulletin*, Issue 12, June/July

Nicoll, A and Atkins, R (1999) 'British defence merger upsets Bonn's vision', *Financial Times*, 19 February

Nicoll, A (2000a) 'Spend more on defence', *Financial Times*, 8 June

Nicoll, A (2000b) 'Thomson and Raytheon discuss link', *Financial Times*, 29 June

Nicoll, A (2000c) 'BAE Chairman calls for strategy for naval yards', *Financial Times*, 15 September

Nicoll, A (2000d) 'Lockheed says Pentagon must lift payments', *Financial Times*, 13 March

Odell, M (2000) 'Pentagon puts UK on spot over missile deal', *Financial Times*, 10 March

Proctor, P (2000) 'A3xx Launch and Lots More', *Aviation Week*, 25 July

Rapson Report (2000) 'New missions for European armed forces and the collective capabilities required for their implementation- reply to the annual report of Council', document 1687, Assembly of Western European Union, forty-sixth session

Robertson, G (1997) 'Review to create fair and efficient defence policy', *Parliamentary Monitor*, September

Robertson, G (1997) 'Armed and Ready', *Tribune*, 12 September

Robertson G (1998) 'Insurance Policy' *Defence Review*, Autumn

Robertson, Lord (2000) 'A new transatlantic bargain', *The House Magazine*, 10 April

Robinson, P (2000) 'Does the Government really have a regional policy?', *The New Regionalism*, Manchester: Centre for Local Economic Strategies, March

Rolls-Royce, (1999) *Annual Report*

SBAC (1999a) UK Aerospace Facts and Figures', pp22-23, London: SBAC

SBAC (1999b) 'SBAC Supply Chain Research Project: Phase One Report', London: SBAC

Schmitt, B (2000), 'From Cooperation to Integration: Defence and Aerospace Industries in Europe', Chaillot Papers 40, July, Paris: WEU Institute for Security Studies

Sloan, S (2000), 'The United States and European Defence', Chaillot Papers 39, April, Paris: WEU Institute for Security Studies

Sharp, J ed (1996) 'About Turn, Forward March with Europe', London: IPPR/Rivers Oram Press

Swedish Ministry of Defence (1999), 'Defence policy bill: A Changing World- A Reformed Defence', 3 August press release

Titley, G (1998) 'Working Document on the communication from the Commission "Implementing European Union defence strategy on defence-related industries", COM(97)0583', PE 226.460, European Parliament Committee on Foreign Affairs, Security and Defence Policy, 28 May, Brussels: European Parliament

Tindemans, L (1997) 'Draft report on the formulation of persepectives for the common security policy of the European Union', PE 217.532/A/rev.2, Brussels: European Parliament

Tindemans, L (1997) 'Draft report on the gradual establishment of a common defence policy for the European Union', Committee on Foreign Affairs, Security and Defence Policy, PE 224.862/A, Brussels: European Parliament

Truscott, P (2000) 'Tackling European defence dilemmas', *The House Magazine*, 10 July

Truscott, P (1999) 'European Defence Co-operation in the 21st Century', 4 March, Brussels: European Parliamentary Labour Party

Truscott, P (1998) 'Long time coming', *Defence Review*, Spring edition

Truscott, P (1997a) *Russia First: Breaking with the West*, London: I.B. Taurus

Truscott, P (1997b) 'Britain's Strategic Defence Review : An EPLP Discussion Paper', 25 September, Brussels: European Parliamentary Labour Party (lodged in House of Commons Library)

Truscott, P (1985) 'The Korean War in British Foreign and Domestic Policy, 1950-1952' D.Phil thesis, Bodleian Library, Oxford (unpublished)

Vincent (1997) Field Marshal Lord, *Foundations for our security in a changing world*, London: Lloyds TSB Forum

Vipotnik, M (1999) 'Sweden to make cuts in defence spending', *Financial Times*, 21 October

Washington Summit Communique (1999a) *An Alliance for the 21st Century*, NATO Press Release, NAC-S(99)64

Washington Summit Communique (1999b) *The Alliance's Strategic Concept*, NATO press release, NAC-S(99)65, 24 April 1999

Willett, S (1997) 'The Eurofighter Debate: A British Perspective', Brussels: International Security Information Service